Leila Khaled

Revolutionary Lives

Series Editors: Brian Doherty, Keele University; Sarah Irving, University of Edinburgh; and Professor Paul Le Blanc, La Roche College, Pittsburgh

Revolutionary Lives is a book series of short introductory critical biographies of radical political figures. The books are sympathetic but not sycophantic, and the intention is to present a balanced and where necessary critical evaluation of the individual's place in their political field, putting their actions and achievements in context and exploring issues raised by their lives, such as the use or rejection of violence, nationalism, or gender in political activism. While individuals are the subject of the books, their personal lives are dealt with lightly except in so far as they mesh with political issues. The focus of these books is the contribution their subjects have made to history, an examination of how far they achieved their aims in improving the lives of the oppressed and exploited, and how they can continue to be an inspiration for many today.

Published titles:

Leila Khaled: Icon of Palestinian Liberation
Sarah Irving

Jean Paul Marat: Tribune of the French Revolution
Clifford D. Conner

Gerrard Winstanley: The Digger's Life and Legacy
John Gurney

www.revolutionarylives.co.uk

Leila Khaled

Icon of Palestinian Liberation

Sarah Irving

PlutoPress
www.plutobooks.com

First published 2012 by Pluto Press
345 Archway Road, London N6 5AA

www.plutobooks.com

Distributed in the United States of America exclusively by
Palgrave Macmillan, a division of St. Martin's Press LLC,
175 Fifth Avenue, New York, NY 10010

British Library Cataloguing in Publication Data
A catalogue record for this book is available from the British Library

ISBN   978 0 7453 2952 9   Hardback
ISBN   978 0 7453 2951 2   Paperback
ISBN   978 1 84964 673 4   PDF
ISBN   978 1 84964 675 8   Kindle
ISBN   978 1 84964 674 1   ePub

Library of Congress Cataloging in Publication Data applied for

This book is printed on paper suitable for recycling and made from fully
managed and sustained forest sources. Logging, pulping and manufacturing
processes are expected to conform to the environmental standards of the
country of origin.

10   9   8   7   6   5   4   3   2

Typeset from disk by Stanford DTP Services, Northampton, England
Simultaneously printed digitally by CPI Antony Rowe, Chippenham, UK and
Edwards Bros in the United States of America

*For three generations of
amazing women—Meg, Cathy, Leila and Merryn*

And for Marc, Zoë and Viv

Contents

List of Illustrations

Acknowledgements

My thanks to Leila Khaled, Khalil Meqdisi, Linda Clair, Naim, Samer and the many other people, especially in Palestine and in the Palestinian diaspora, who didn't want their names made public but who have shared their time, memories, thoughts, and hospitality with me; to all the Palestinians living under military occupation or separated from their homeland, whose steadfastness and courage should be an inspiration to all who believe in justice; to David Castle at Pluto Press for his immense patience; and to the International Solidarity Movement, for luring me to Palestine in the first place.

Introduction

August 29, 1969. A young woman, wearing a white suit, sunhat and big shades sits at Rome airport, awaiting flight TWA 840. She looks nervous—but then so do many imminent flyers. But this Audrey Hepburn lookalike in her summer outfit has smuggled a gun and hand grenades past airport security, and is pretending not to know the man across the room. He is Salim Issawi, a fellow combatant of the "Che Guevara Commando Unit" of the Popular Front for the Liberation of Palestine (al-Jabhah al-Sha'biyyah li Tahrir Filastin). She is Leila Khaled. She is evasive but amiable to the fellow passenger trying to chat her up.

Leila Khaled and Salim Issawi force the plane to divert from its course to Athens and fly over Khaled's birthplace, Haifa, a city which as a Palestinian refugee she can no longer visit. Scaring but not harming the terrified passengers, the plane is ordered to head for Damascus where its nose cone is blown up. The press are intrigued by the "girl hijacker," but months after the hijacking, Khaled is berated by the PFLP's leader, George Habash, for refusing to speak to TV crews. Instead, she goes under the knife, undergoing six sessions of plastic surgery. She knows that more missions have been planned for her, and she doesn't want to be recognizable.

September 6, 1970. Another young couple, travelling on Honduran passports, board an El Al Boeing 707 at Amsterdam. The man is Patrick Arguello, a Nicaraguan-American member of the Sandinista movement which nine years later will liberate Nicaragua from the dictator Somoza. The woman is, again, Leila Khaled.

The couple sit demurely in the second row of the tourist-class section of the plane, which is bound for New York. But as it heads over the English Channel, they try to force their way into the cockpit. Across Europe and the Middle East, several other airplanes are also being hijacked by teams from the PFLP, but this is the only

The iconic image of Leila Khaled: The *Guardian's* Katharine Viner summed it up as: '[T]he picture which made her the symbol of Palestinian resistance and female power: the gun held in fragile hands, the shiny hair wrapped in a keffiah, the delicate Audrey Hepburn face refusing to meet your eye.' (AFP/Getty Images)

plane where things go badly wrong for the assailants. The plane's pilot uses a nosedive to throw the hijackers off balance, Arguello is shot dead, and Khaled is captured.

Khaled and Arguello intended to join their comrades at Dawson's Field, a defunct British RAF base in Jordan where the rest of the planes will spend the coming weeks, embroiled in an international incident which nearly plunges Jordan into civil war and stretches the already tense Middle East almost to breaking point. Instead, Leila Khaled spends the next month in London's Ealing police station.

*   *   *

Despite her indisputable involvement in the hijackings, the prisoner exchange which eventually took place meant that Leila Khaled has never faced charges. She has been one of the best known Palestinian women, but has been condemned by some feminists for using the welfare of her nation's women to promote a left-wing or nationalist political position. To some she is the glamorous icon of women revolutionaries, to others a heroic fighter for her country's liberation, and to yet more a notorious terrorist to be vilified in the press and excluded from nations she seeks to visit. Her own sister, mistaken for her, was assassinated, but she remained committed to her political course. Leila Khaled's life has run alongside the history of the modern State of Israel, in a condition of mutual hostility, and has been greatly shaped by the country she was forced to leave as a small child.

Leila Khaled's public image has been almost entirely dictated by her great moment in history, the defining hijackings of 1969 and 1970. But since then she has been a wife and mother, a teacher and campaigner, a member of the Palestinian National Council and a leader in the General Union of Palestinian Women. Like many militants and those labeled "terrorists," from Northern Ireland to Nicaragua, she has moved from the armed struggle to the political arena, although she still says she would die for her country. Her iconic status has opened doors and made people listen to her, but it has also excluded her—from countries who deny her entry and from people for whom she will always be no more or less than a terrorist.

Although Leila Khaled was allowed to visit Britain in spring 2002 for a number of speaking engagements, the fact that she has since been denied a visa illustrates the passions she still arouses. I first met Leila on her 2002 visit, at a small gathering at the Pankhurst Women's Centre in Manchester. I had recently returned from working in the West Bank, during the Israeli army's most ferocious attacks for years. President Arafat had been held captive in his own headquarters in Ramallah, while dozens of civilians from homes around Bethlehem's Manger Square had endured six weeks' siege in the Church of the Nativity, after they fled there alongside fighters taking cover from invading Israeli troops. In Jenin, an unknown number of families had been bulldozed into the rubble of their own homes, while the ancient city of Nablus had witnessed the destruction of historic buildings by Israeli forces trying to flush out armed Palestinians.

In this heightened atmosphere, the chair of the meeting pointed me out to Leila, who crossed the room, brought me to my feet and embraced me, saying that she wanted to smell and touch her homeland on someone who had visited it so recently.

Then in her late fifties, Leila Khaled was still a very striking woman, recognizable from the 30-year-old photos of the beautiful young hijacker. At a public meeting at Manchester's Friends Meeting House, she held a crowd of 150 spellbound as she talked, not about her own personal glory days, but about the ongoing struggle of the Palestinian people for recognition and rights. She had a deep, throaty voice, exacerbated by chain-smoking, and an iconoclastic attitude.

She explained to a group of us around a restaurant table that she was from a Muslim culture, and the importance of this in the identities of all Palestinians, even those who were not Muslims. She then informed me that, as a young woman, I should understand that the great pleasures of life were good food, good drink and good love, but that she was inclined to add cigarettes to this list. I'm not sure what I was expecting of this woman who had hijacked not one but two passenger jets for the Palestinian cause, but I was fairly sure that this wasn't it.

Oddly little has been written about Leila Khaled. Like modern-day footballers and pop singers, she published an autobiography before she was even 30, in 1973. This was ghost-written by George Hajjar, an academic who then worked for the PFLP's publicity department, in order to take political advantage of the events of 1970; according to Leila Khaled, she would spend her days dictating her life story to Hajjar, and he would return each written chapter to her to be agreed upon. It has long been out of print, and copies in good condition now change hands for hundreds of pounds. Also capitalizing on these events was a tabloidese paperback, *Leila's Hijack War*, co-authored by that doyen of British election-night coverage, Peter Snow, and containing more information about the experiences of British hijack victims than about those of Leila herself. Eileen

MacDonald's 1990 book on "women terrorists," *Shoot the Women First*, carried a chapter on Leila, based partly on an interview done when she was still living in Yarmouk refugee camp in Damascus. Apart from these books, English speakers wanting to know more about this remarkable woman have had little to go on except for a few interviews in publications including the *Guardian*, left-wing magazines, and, with an impeccable but twisted logic, *Aviation Security International*.

This book tries to at least partly fill the gap left by this paucity of information. It is based on a series of interviews carried out with Leila Khaled in Amman, where she now lives, in 2008, as well as other interviews, books, and articles, both hostile towards and supportive of her beliefs and actions. As well as recording the events of Leila Khaled's own life, I wanted to explore (within the limitations of a short book) some of the issues and passions she arouses: how do militants whose careers start with violent action end them in the arena of political negotiation and discussion? Why, and how, do people—especially women—decide to follow the path of armed struggle, and what do they gain and lose? How does the left-wing revolution of Khaled's day link to the Islamist parties which dominate the armed Palestinian resistance of today? And how does the romanticized, sexualized figure of the "Audrey Hepburn terrorist" fit into the wider Palestinian struggle?

* * *

When Leila Khaled hijacked her first plane, the Popular Front for the Liberation of Palestine was a left-wing organization with international links and the declared intention of winning the return of the Palestinian people to the lands they had left only 20 years before. This was the era of Che Guevara, killed in Bolivia just two years earlier, and of liberation struggles in South East Asia. The right of oppressed peoples to resist by armed means was discussed worldwide, and the heroes of these movements decorated the walls of student bedrooms and left-wing homes. The second wave of feminism was also breaking, adding another aspect to the environment in which news of this young female hijacker would be received.

In Leila's Middle East home, Israel had just defeated the combined armies of Egypt, Jordan, and Syria in the Six Day War, humiliating the Arab world militarily and capturing the remaining Palestinian territories west of the River Jordan and north of the Sinai. Palestinians in the West Bank and Gaza, including thousands of refugees from the initial establishment of the State of Israel in 1948, had been living under Jordanian and Egyptian rule, but were now subject to Israeli military occupation. Despite this, the world's attention to the Palestinians themselves was minimal. They were seen by the West as a small, dispossessed refugee people, caught up in the hostility between Jews and Arabs in the Middle East, and of little importance except as an excuse for aggression by Arab powers.

Amongst the Palestinians of the refugee camps of Jordan, Lebanon, and Syria, discontent had been brewing. A resistance movement, which had been growing since the mid 1960s, had been further radicalized and popularized by the Six Day War and by Palestinians' increasing suspicion of the hollow support voiced by Arab regimes. As Rosemary Sayigh, who lived in Lebanon throughout the 1970s, puts it:

It is difficult to separate out the Palestinian Resistance Movement (PRM) from the historical moment and mood in which it first arose, soon after the Six Day War, like a phoenix out of ashes, galvanising a whole nation humiliated by the collapse of the Arab armies. In this first glamorous début, the Resistance reaped a harvest of hero-worship from a wide spectrum of Arab public opinion, salon nationalists going so far as to call the fedayeen "angels" and "saviours." This kind of support soon showed its shallowness, but for a time it put pressure on the Arab regimes to give the PRM official backing ... by setting itself squarely in the framework of Third World struggle against US economic and political domination, the PRM revitalised radical elements in the Arab world and exposed the real character of the [reactionary Arab] regimes.[1]

If the 1969 hijacking had made Leila Khaled famous for a few weeks, the audacity and scale of her 1970 enterprise extended her notoriety to new heights. The deliberate explosion of the four hijacked planes which had reached Dawson's Field in Jordan, the confrontation between the Palestinian resistance and the Jordanian army, which almost tipped the country into civil war, and the involvement of Syria, Israel, the USSR, and the USA, brought the world to a state of extreme tension. For the Palestinian people, the events heralded greater repression in Jordan and the expulsion of militants to Lebanon, and, after further conflict there, on to Tunis and the wider diaspora.

For Khaled, the events of 1970 meant that her image joined that of Che Guevara on thousands of left-wing walls, and to many she became the archetype of the female revolutionary and the Palestinian woman. This notoriety was to have significant consequences for her, and for the way she and her cause have been regarded. Leila's actions are still remembered precisely because they were so extraordinary. But because they have caught memories and imaginations, they have come to represent elements of Palestinian and left-wing identity far beyond themselves. Leila Khaled's actions have impacted on the way that Palestinians as a people have been viewed by the world for the past 35 years, and have ensured that she looms large in discussions of women, the Middle East, and the tactics of liberation struggles.

As feminist writer Robin Morgan states, in the eyes of many in the West, "there are two well-fostered stereotypes of the Palestinian woman: she is a grenade-laden Leila Khaled or she is an illiterate refugee willingly producing sons for the revolution."[2] This generalization may say more about Western perceptions than Palestinian reality, but it does illustrate the extent to which Leila Khaled joined a small pantheon of individuals who, along with Yasser Arafat and assorted suicide bombers, spring to the minds of many Westerners when Palestine is mentioned. This is a distinctly ambivalent thing, for Leila and for her people. It means that even before they became associated with suicide bombing as an instrument of struggle, Palestinians were irrevocably linked with terrorism.

Some, including Leila Khaled, insist on the Palestinians' right to defend themselves through armed struggle. Others—including those sympathetic to the broad Palestinian cause—see the use of high-profile violence as playing straight into Israeli hands, and as obscuring the grind (and often non-violent resistance) of the day-to-day survival of those Palestinians living under occupation or in the poverty and discrimination of the refugee camps. Does Leila's high profile turn the Palestinian struggle into something glamorous, full of clandestine meetings and international plots? Or does it obscure the everyday resistance of ordinary people, like the tax refusal with which the townspeople of Beit Sahour in the West Bank defied the Israeli occupation? On internet sites, grotesque male bloggers celebrate Leila as the "ultimate badass feminist revolutionary chick with a gun," objectifying Leila and her comrades while reveling in their own radicalism.[3]

For some feminists and activists, Leila's role as a high-profile woman who has been so prominent in the "man's world" of armed political struggle has made her a thrilling, inspiring figure. Some women, especially black feminists, identify her along with figures such as Black Panther Assata Shakur as a woman "living" their resistance in parallel with those working in the domains of theory and discussion.[4] Professor Eileen Kuttab of the West Bank's Birzeit University described fighters such as Leila as having "tied the national liberation struggle to their struggle for social liberation,"[5] and as having won a position for women that meant that when the First Intifada started in the later 1980s, women were seen as equal partners in the struggle.

For others, however, her adoption of "male" methods of violence, and her history of work within male-dominated organizations has illustrated that, like Margaret Thatcher or Condoleezza Rice, she has put her fellow women second and "sold out" to patriarchal interests. Robin Morgan's work on gender and violence, *The Demon Lover*, roundly criticizes Leila for obeying a macho ethos of terrorism and betraying the needs of Palestinian women. According to Morgan, Leila Khaled "has not survived being female. [E]ven for the unattached woman, the gestures of obeisance [to male authority], the protestations of denial, must be made. The woman who rebels via the male mode can do so only to the point where her own rebellion might begin."[6]

Morgan notes that when she carried out the hijackings, Leila "was young, she looked like Audrey Hepburn, and she was the first 'female terrorist' to hit the news in mid-action; the press had a field day."[7] In acknowledging the press images and stereotypes of Leila, though, Morgan never seems to note that her own response to Leila, and those of many other Western academics and commentators, is based on those stereotypes. Are the "obeisances" which Morgan condemns a recognition of the constraints placed on women wanting a public role in Arab society? Khaled complains of this very fact in her autobiography, which Morgan ignores. Despite the flaws in Morgan's reasoning, her view is not unusual, and there are many in the women's and peace movements who see figures such as Leila and Che as working within the frameworks of the oppression they seek to overcome.

Nevertheless, to many Leila Khaled is still a figure of admiration, fascination, and inspiration. In the world of reality TV, X Factor, and American Idol, this presents a certain challenge. How to celebrate the charismatic and extraordinary individual whilst avoiding the cult of celebrity, and emphasizing the context that makes political "heroes" what they are? And in a world of horrific violence, where civilians are increasingly on the receiving end of conflict and struggle, it's a fine line to tread acknowledging courage and commitment to a political cause without glorifying and glamourizing tactics used out of necessity and desperation.

Is it politically acceptable to focus on individual "heroes"? I think it is, in the sense that there are individuals whose lives and examples might have things—good or bad—to teach us about personal paths through political struggle. And I think it is acceptable for individuals engaged in political activity to be inspired by well-known (or more obscure) figures, as long as they also acknowledge that these are not saints or gods but people of their specific time and place. This book, and the series of which it is one of the first, will seek to tread that fine line.

1

Haifa, Lebanon, Kuwait

Leila Khaled was born on April 9, 1944 in the port city of Haifa. Her family were comfortable, members of the lower middle class. Her father, Ali Khaled, was a café owner, running a business he had built up over 20 years, and her mother looked after the growing family. She was the sixth child of an eventual dozen, the last of whom, her brother Nasser, was not born until 12 years later, when the family were refugees in the town of Tyre (Sour) in Lebanon.

Modern-day Haifa is often held up by Israel, in its efforts to demonstrate its multi-ethnic credentials to a Western audience, as a model of Arab-Jewish co-existence. Like many cities in Palestine it has a long history of Muslim, Christian, and Jewish communities living side-by-side in some degree of harmony; whilst on one hand modern Haifa is home to a vibrant Palestinian cultural life and a number of joint Palestinian-Jewish projects, on the other its contemporary Palestinian population is subject to the same social and economic discrimination and political marginalization as other "Arab Israelis." In 1854 Haifa had a small Jewish community (32 of its 2,012 residents), while 1,200 were Muslim and the remainder Christians—mainly of the Orthodox denomination to which most Palestinian Christians historically belong, but also a small number of Catholics and Protestants.[1]

In 1911 Haifa was still "predominantly Arab," but Jewish settlements started to grow in the area by the early 1920s, several of them funded by the Jewish National Fund and by American Zionist organizations.[2] By 1929, tensions throughout Palestine, spurred by increasing Zionist settlement and a deteriorating global economic situation, led the British Mandate authorities to fear that Haifa was one of the towns where attacks on Jewish and British targets might happen.[3] During the Great Arab Revolt of 1936–9 against the British Mandate authorities and Zionist immigration, Haifa's Palestinian and Jewish residents were driven further apart: in July 1938 two Jewish terrorist bombs killed over 60 Palestinians, while Arab employees of Jewish companies and several Jews were wounded or killed by Palestinians.[4]

From the small town of about 2,000 people in the 1850s, Haifa had become a major city. The British Mandate authorities had developed it in preference to the ancient port of Akka and it was the final point of an oil pipeline which carried Iraqi oil for export to Europe and of a spur of the Hejaz railway which linked it to Damascus.[5] As a prosperous urban center, it attracted large numbers of Jewish immigrants during the 1930s, as well as a substantial Palestinian middle class who later, as refugees, played a large role in building up cities such as Amman as major cultural and economic centers in the Middle East.[6]

But by 1946 the animosity between the new Jewish communities in Palestine and the Palestinian inhabitants was starting to be felt in Haifa. In 1946 the Palmach, an underground Jewish militia, attacked the train yards in Haifa, resulting in major reprisals by the British Mandate authorities and the arrest of 3,000 Zionist activists across Palestine.[7] By late 1947 the Irgun, another Zionist armed force, had started to attack Arab villages around Haifa and Arab supporters had started to retaliate with attacks on Jewish areas.[8] The Palestinian population was nervous of the large Jewish contingent in the area; they felt cut off from other major Arab towns and hemmed in by a growing circle of Jewish settler towns and kibbutzim.[9] Hearing the news of violence across the rest of Palestine—including the April 9 massacre at Deir Yassin—the Khaled family fled on April 13, 1948.

As the situation across Palestine spiraled out of control in April 1948, Haifa descended into confusion. British forces withdrew to the port area on April 21 and within 48 hours the Haganah—the military force which later became the Israeli army—had taken the city. What happened then is a subject of debate: the Palestinian chief magistrate and militia commander had left on the first night of attack to "seek reinforcements," but apparently never returned. On April 22 the local Arab leadership told the population to stay,[10] as did the Jewish mayor, but the Arab High Command in Damascus told them to flee because they were planning to bomb the Jewish forces.[11] The local Arab leadership changed its mind and told its people to leave and many fled, spurred on by "rough treatment" from the Irgun and Haganah, including forcible evictions, house to house searches, detentions and beatings. By May 1st only 3–4,000 Palestinians were left in Haifa.[12]

Despite the growing tensions between Palestinians and Jews in Haifa, Leila Khaled's memories and autobiography record a happy beginning to her childhood, with fairly liberal and indulgent parents who allowed the high-spirited child to run her own writ. Khaled insists that one of her early memories is of a Jewish friend, a little girl called Tamara, who still features in Khaled's talks about her life and her feelings about relations between Jews and Muslims. She also records that her family's relations with the inhabitants of the nearby Jewish quarter of Haifa, Hadar, were fairly cordial until November 1947, when tensions increased after the UN partitioning of Palestine and Israel. "The turning-point in my relationship with Tamara," wrote Khaled in 1973, "came on November 29, 1947, when the UN partitioned Palestine between Tamara and me. Tamara was awarded 56% of my land. I was expected to accede to this demand and congratulate Tamara's people."[13]

Khaled's family fled Haifa when she was just four, so her memories are vague, she says, and they quickly degenerate into a child's hazy recollections of unrest and confusion. "I was too young, but I do remember some little things," she says. "I remember a staircase, because when there were clashes on the street in the area we used to run and crouch under it. It was wooden and there was a banister. And once there was no electricity and one of our relatives came and told my mother there was a curfew and I was wondering, what is a curfew? I thought that the cut off electricity was the curfew. I used to say it in a crooked way and everybody was laughing at me."

And in memories which would resonate with later events, Khaled already noted that "all the time we were afraid, especially because my father was often not at home and sometimes I heard him coming in late at night and then going. I don't even remember how he was at that time."

Since 1948, the 9th of April, Leila Khaled's birthday, has been held as a day of mourning by the Palestinian people. On this date, over a hundred of the 750 inhabitants of the village of Deir Yassin, outside Jerusalem, were massacred by members of the Irgun and Stern Gang, militias whose bloody bombings and campaign of violence against Palestinian communities include some of the most shameful episodes in the story of the establishment of the State of Israel.[14] In her 1973 autobiography, Khaled records that her birthday was never celebrated after she turned four. She also wrote that on April 11 she saw her first dead body: "I do remember being terrified, but I do not remember whether the dead person was Arab or Jew. I only remember hearing bombs exploding and seeing the blood spurting from the dying man's stomach. I hid under the staircase and stared at the corpse in the street outside. I trembled and wondered whether this would be the fate of my father."[15]

Leila Khaled's mother and siblings were amongst some of the earlier Palestinians to flee Haifa, on April 13, 1948 (just four days after Leila's fourth birthday), after several days of shooting and shelling in the city. Her mother had hired a car to take them to an uncle's house in Tyre, but tried to hang on as long as possible in the hope that they would not have to leave. The departure was also delayed when her mother tried to help move the body of another man killed by the shelling in front of their house. When the time finally came to go, Leila herself had to be dragged out from her hiding-place under the stairs by one of her sisters.

"I remember the kitchen and that I loved dates," Khaled recalls. "My father had bought us a big round basket of dates. My mother said we had to go to Lebanon, and we used to go every year to Lebanon so that's not unusual. But when they were ready to go my mother counted us and found somebody missing. It was me. I was hiding under the staircase and I heard my mother and the neighbors calling and I didn't answer. The car was waiting and someone found me in the little space by the door, hiding with the basket of dates." She was, she remembers, afraid that the dates would be left behind.

But the child Leila's fear for her basket of fruit saved the family's life. The car which had left without them as she hid was shelled just a short distance down the road and two small girls were killed. "Don't scream at Leila," the neighbors told her mother, "she saved your lives." But the second time they tried to leave, Leila's mother made sure that she was the first to be taken out to the car, carrying her baby sister. One of her older brothers had already gone ahead to Beirut. The child Leila "was crying because my mother was crying. Before when we were preparing to go to Lebanon we were happy, but this time everybody was crying."

Khaled also recalls that her mother later told her that one of their neighbors, a Jewish woman, urged them not to leave and invited them to stay in her house until it was safe. But, she says, "At that time the Deir Yassin massacre was in everybody's mind and so everybody was afraid of other massacres. I think the Zionists spread rumors to exaggerate it to make people afraid."

"All the way from Haifa we were stuffed in the car," Leila Khaled remembers. The journey was short—less than two hours, she thinks. But they witnessed other refugees walking the long distance into exile, and Khaled's father wasn't with the family. He had apparently stayed in Haifa, intending to keep his home and business and to invite his family back once the bloodshed was over. But on April 22 both house and shop were seized.[16] He later joined the Palestinian resistance and, in the wake of the Arab defeat, was sent to Gaza and then Egypt before finally making his way back to his family a year later.

Of their first months in Lebanon, Khaled records that she "recall[s] nothing besides accompanying my older sisters Nawal, Zakiah and Rahaab to the United Nations Relief & Works Agency (UNRWA) provision bureau to collect our miserable rations. My sisters were humiliated; my mother was angry."[17]

The family spent nearly a year in Tyre, a time Leila Khaled remembers as one of exile and dispossession. She told Eileen MacDonald that: "my uncle's house was surrounded by a large garden with lots of orange trees. As children at home we had always picked our oranges when we were hungry. My mother slapped our hands and said those oranges are not yours and you are not allowed to eat them. Since then, I haven't been able to eat oranges. It brings such a feeling of sadness to me to see them and to think that our orange trees are still there in Haifa, but now they belong to somebody else."[18]

Leila Khaled acknowledges that her family was better off than the majority of Palestinian refugees. They had relatives to stay with in Tyre and were spared some of the worst experiences of those who had nowhere to go but the UNRWA camps. But, she says, it was still a difficult transition from the comfortable conditions of her first four years, and this laid the foundations for the politicization of her teens.

"At home, Palestinian families were in a miserable state," she says. "Whatever we asked for was rejected by our parents, especially our mother, because our father often wasn't there. Whenever we asked 'why?' the answer was: because you are not in Palestine. All the deprivation we lived in, it was because we 'are not in Palestine.' When we grew up this idea became politicized—that we won't have anything unless we return to Palestine. So the idea of return began at home because it was the answer for everything, and we had to know why it happened this way and who was responsible. Sometimes people accused us of leaving our homes just because we are afraid and there were even rumors that some Palestinians sold their land, and that was humiliating for us."

The stain of the accusation that they had sold their homes to the Israelis and fled was one which, Khaled recounts, lasted for decades. In 1982, during the Israeli invasion of Lebanon, Khaled was working with one of the Palestinian women's organizations which tried to find housing and supplies for the refugees who fled north to the sectarian hell that was Beirut.

"I went into an empty building, a new one, in Beirut and I heard a woman telling another one, 'you see now why we left our homes? For years and years you were telling us that we sold our lands and homes.' I entered and asked what they were discussing. There was a woman sitting there with her children and another woman sitting here with her children, one Palestinian and the other Lebanese. And the Palestinian woman was saying, like she wanted to retaliate, 'see how people are made to live?' She said this woman had been saying for 20 or 30 years that the Palestinians got what they deserved because they sold their land, that she made us feel guilty, that every Palestinian should feel guilty for running away."

* * *

A bright, "boyish and aggressive" child, Khaled was soon sent to kindergarten to keep her out of trouble. It was, she describes in her 1973 autobiography, largely a "babysitting affair," where the only structured activity was learning to recite the Holy Koran. She progressed at the age of six to the Evangelical Churches' School for the Palestinians, a charity school where she rebelled against being put in the first grade because of her poor English (instead of the second year, which her age warranted). With typical bravado, she considered her skills in Arabic and mathematics to warrant being put up to grade four.[19]

Leila Khaled's introduction to formal Arab nationalist politics came via her older brothers and sisters. Six of the boys and girls in the Khaled family became involved with the Arab Nationalist Movement (ANM), the organization founded by George Habash and Wadi'a Haddad while they were students at the American University of Beirut (AUB).

"My oldest brother was studying at AUB, where all the leaders of the ANM were studying" recalls Khaled. "And in our families the oldest boy has the same authority as the father and has a special status, and within the ANM it was believed that every member of the Movement should influence his family first, so my brother influenced my two older sisters and my other brother who was two years older than me. Then my sisters influenced me." She was only eight years old when Mohammed, her 17-year-old eldest brother, started debating politics with his father, exciting the little Leila. Gradually, she began to realize that there were larger forces behind the fact that she and her friends had to go to school in the big, draughty tent which housed the first two grades at the Union of Evangelical Churches School for Palestinians. In December 1952 a winter storm blew the tent over, injuring several children and terrifying the rest.

Politicization on the subject of Palestinian dispossession was one thing, but applying its lessons to other injustices was initially beyond her. Being beaten in class by Samirah, a "scum of earth" girl from a refugee camp, was another turning point. When nine-year-old Leila was caught bullying the camp girl, their teacher lectured her on the fact that the peasants eking out an existence in the camps were the "real" Palestinians, who had been connected to the land for centuries, unlike her own middle-class urban parents. For the Khaled family themselves, conditions were slowly improving and in 1955, when Leila was 11, they moved into a three-room apartment and "hunger was no longer a threat."[20]

But, says Khaled, the older Khaled children all remained politically active. "Generally the whole atmosphere at that time was of rising nationalist feeling in the Arab world, especially after Nasser came to power in Egypt." For Leila Khaled, her siblings, and the refugee community surrounding them, the upswing in Arab nationalism was a way out of the sense of helplessness which pervaded their society after the Nakba, or Disaster, as Palestinians call the founding of the State of Israel. The youngest Khaled brother was born in 1956 and named Nasser after the Egyptian president who had faced down the West over the Suez Canal. Later, Khaled joked that "Now the family could either form a soccer team or take on the 'twelve tribes' of Israel. The decision was already made. That autumn was the most exciting period of my childhood."[21]

"Every Palestinian who lived through the Nakba felt they had to do something," Khaled recalls. "At school we used to go on demonstrations, always, on three dates. Even when we were very young we learnt the 15th of May,[22] the 2nd of November, and the 29th of November. November 2nd was the Balfour Declaration[23] and the 29th was the UN resolution on the partition of Palestine. I'm not exaggerating, at school every child knew on these dates we have to go demonstrating. All the teachers were Palestinian and they taught us what the dates meant." Nabil, Leila's own teacher at the age of nine or ten, was also a political activist who spoke at Palestinian rallies, and she hero-worshipped him.[24]

In 1958, however, conflict broke out in Lebanon. The Lebanese population was—and is—religiously diverse, split between Maronite and other Christian denominations, Sunni and Shia Muslims, and Druze, whose faith is an offshoot of Ismaili Islam found in Lebanon, Jordan, Syria, and Palestine/Israel. In an effort to maintain a balance between the sometimes warring faiths, the 1943 Lebanese National Pact specified that offices such as the president, prime minister and speaker of the national parliament are allocated to particular confessional groups. But, some believe, rather than detaching religion from Lebanese politics, the constitutional framework has entrenched communal divisions.[25]

In the late 1950s, President Camille Chamoun—a Maronite who had been elected with the support of the Druze leader Kamal Jumblatt—decided to support the USA's "Eisenhower Doctrine." The Christian leader saw US support as a counterweight to the power and popularity of Egyptian president Nasser and of his supporters, including the pan-Arab secularists of the ANM, and the perceived threat of the United Arab Republic which Syria and Egypt, at the height of pan-Arab fervor, had formed in February 1958. (As left-wing Indian writer R. K. Karanjia put it in 1959, "The basic principles of the Eisenhower Doctrine were outlined in the memorandum which Dulles sent to Eisenhower at the close of 1956 and which appeared in the European press the next spring ... Dulles wrote that if America failed to act vigorously at the time, she would never be able to fulfill the mission to which God had entrusted her of guiding the free world. He believed that the US should adopt a new policy aimed, above all, at checking the growth of Arab nationalism and at filling the vacuum in West Asia.")

Chamoun's reaction to the ascendancy of secular pan-Arabism added to tensions rising from accusations of fraud during the 1957 elections, which had allegedly stripped Sunni and Druze parties of seats. Riots broke out, the USA and Britain readied their troops, and Lebanese air force planes strafed Muslim positions in Beirut. Both Christians and Muslims were the victims of targeted assassinations.[26] The Arab Nationalist Movement, with which members of the Khaled family had already allied themselves, had received arms and other support from the Ba'ath regime over the border in Syria, but was a minor political and military player in the wider turmoil.[27]

For the 14-year-old Leila Khaled, the conflict showed "how much more there was to the movement than writing, distributing pamphlets, demonstrating or making speeches."[28] It was a way of proving her commitment to the cause. She wasn't allowed to fight, but along with other children was given the dangerous task of carrying food, balanced on their heads, to the fighters on the front line. "We had about ten kilos of flour at home and I decided that I could bake enough bread for the men. But instead of baking it I kneaded the entire ten kilos and fried the dough in olive oil. Now I could supply a regiment," wrote Khaled in 1973. "The crucial part was when I delivered the bread to the lines ... I was amazed by the speed of the bullets as they buzzed by, and was somehow surprised to see a real battle scene raging, particularly with me in its midst. Until then I had thought that battles were like demonstrations. I screamed to both sides to stop shooting because I only had bread on my tray which I carried on the top of my head as befits a Palestinian maiden."[29]

Khaled's bravery was the ticket which allowed her to join the Arab Nationalist Movement as a full member once the fighting was over.[30] But the war also gave her a taste of just how serious her political commitment had to be, when local nationalist leader Maan Halawah was shot by Lebanese gendarmes while Khaled stood just a few feet away, handing him stones to hurl. She was one of the demonstrators who helped to bundle him in a car, and was waiting at the hospital when the surgeon came out of the operating theatre to announce that Halawah was dead.[31]

In the heightened political atmosphere which prevailed after the intervention of the US Marines and the institution of a precarious peace after the 1958 conflict, Khaled was, despite only being in her mid-teens, active as a full member in the ANM. It was a semi-underground movement whose members often lost university places or were expelled from the country for their involvement. At this point in time, the ANM was firmly a nationalist organization rather than a leftist one; the socialist beliefs which became commonplace amongst revolutionary movements in the 1960s were less prevalent. The Movement was primarily interested in bringing together the various Arab countries in a secular pan-Arab project which would unite the region against US and European imperialism, as seen during the Suez crisis in 1956, and against Zionism and an ethnically exclusive state of Israel. Many of the founding members of the ANM were Palestinian and Palestine was one of its main political priorities, in contrast with the position adopted by some other secular Arab nationalist movements, like the Ba'ath parties, who regarded the defeat of the Palestinians in 1948 as just one of many colonialist interventions in their region, not worth "one letter" of discussion.[32]

Khaled's involvement after the civil war was on a smaller scale than this, but it was still risky. On one occasion, she told journalist Eileen MacDonald, she was stopped by a Lebanese army soldier while distributing illicit ANM leaflets during a military curfew. Convincing him that she was out looking for a midwife to attend to a pregnant neighbor, she not only persuaded him not to arrest her, but had him stand guard while she pushed leaflets under the door of each house, still on the pretext of seeking out medical help.[33]

Khaled had started joining in demonstrations, along with most other Palestinian children, from the age of ten. Heading out onto the streets with the rest of the school was acceptable to her parents, the behavior of a true Palestinian child keeping in touch with her roots and preparing to return to her homeland. Her older brother's tales of the vicious beatings doled out to student protesters against the 1953 visit of US Secretary of State John Foster Dulles to the Middle East only spurred Khaled on further.[34] But when she started getting more involved, joining the ANM and going to political meetings with her sisters, her mother started worrying about their reputations. In the 1950s, Tyre was a more conservative city than cosmopolitan Beirut. But support for the girls' involvement came from a surprising source: their father, who had lost his own health in the battle for Palestine in 1948. "They want their homeland, they should fight for it," he told his wife.

Even though she had her father's backing, at times Khaled had to take desperate measures to get to meetings—including, on one occasion, sneaking out of the house and across town in her nightdress, because her mother had confiscated her clothes in an attempt to keep her at home. She was chastised by her comrades for her unsuitable dress, and slapped by her mother for her shamelessness when she got home.[35] "I was terribly disturbed by [my comrades'] male chauvinism and self-righteousness," she wrote later.[36]

Despite her political involvement and the sectarian tensions simmering around them, Khaled was a bright student who outgrew the Evangelical Churches' educational facilities and was sent to the Saida School to study for her baccalaureate. At the Saida, she encountered a black American teacher, Miss McNight, a student of Martin Luther King's teachings who told her about discrimination and racism in the USA. Miss McNight also, she says, taught the young Leila the difference between Jews and Zionists, making her recall the friendships she had enjoyed with the Jewish children of Hadar and incorporate the idea of Jewish anti-Zionists and its implications into her political thinking.[37] In doing so, McNight seems to have taken Khaled's own views beyond those of the ANM's leadership at the time, which was apparently less sophisticated in differentiating between Jewish people and Zionists.[38]

In 1962 Leila Khaled passed her baccalaureate with flying colors, but for unknown reasons wasn't given the university scholarship that should have accompanied her high marks. With the family giving her brother's degree fees precedence, she managed to talk her oldest brother, who was working in Kuwait, into paying for her, and she registered at AUB with plans to specialize in pharmacy or agriculture. In the hotbed of student radicalism that was the American University of Beirut, Khaled was in her element, throwing herself into political activities far more than the studies this "intellectual graveyard" offered.[39] Already established in the ANM, she also got involved with the General Union of Palestinian Students, which in 1963 was campaigning for support for a popular rebellion aimed at establishing an independent Palestinian republic, based in Jordanian-controlled Nablus. She even managed to persuade the ANM to include her in their first round of military training for student activists, although fellow activists tried to talk her out of it, claiming that she wouldn't be able to withstand the cold weather and hard training, and that anyway she would be an embarrassment just by being there.[40]

Khaled also described in her 1973 autobiography how she enjoyed fierce political debates with her American room-mate, Judy Sinninger, over the Cuban missile crisis and Nasser's dispatch of United Arab Republic troops to Yemen. She also claimed to be "impressed" by Judy's "amorality," signified by her kissing each of her string of boyfriends. Khaled herself admits to few youthful romantic attachments. "For six years, I liked a fellow Palestinian student, of peasant background. At first his careful avoidance of girls provoked my curiosity. Later I discovered his dislike of women stemmed from watching his mother being raped by Israeli soldiers as they were fleeing from the Safad area in 1948 ... I've had casual boyfriends but never really become really attached to any man," she wrote in the early 1970s, apparently before her brief marriage to a PFLP comrade.

After only a year of her degree course Khaled's brother, who was paying her fees as well as helping to support their younger brothers and sisters, announced that he could no longer afford it. Fairly sanguine about her lost education, especially given the contempt she had for the "reactionary" teaching of AUB, Khaled was instead sent to Kuwait to teach English, a comparatively well-paid job which would allow her to send money home. It also allowed her to avoid the possibility that she might be compelled to look for a husband to support her, something she really "was not looking for."[41] "I did not like it but I could not do anything about it, so I had to go," Khaled says. In her autobiography she described al-Jahrah, the Kuwaiti town she eventually found work in, as "the city of eternal boredom."[42]

Khaled managed to keep up her teaching in Kuwait for six years, returning to Lebanon each summer to escape the Gulf's desert heat and to reconnect with her ANM comrades, and then returning for another school year. Her unruliness and refusal to adapt to the authority of head teachers meant that she was often given the younger classes to teach, where it was thought she wouldn't be able to try to indoctrinate her charges with Arab nationalist politics. But she apparently enjoyed the work itself, describing the children of one year as "tireless children who could have out-raced baby camels ... they were a delight to be with."[43]

Working in Kuwait also forced her political involvement underground. Political activity was largely forbidden and the ANM's members had to work in secret. "When I went there I was told, don't say you are in the Arab Nationalist Movement," says Khaled, for whom this was yet another restriction in an alien new environment without cinemas, boyfriends, or any other way to pass the time, where she was almost fired for wearing a short-sleeved top. The consequences of being found out for involvement in Arab nationalist politics would have been dire.[44] "There were Kuwaitis who were members of the ANM too, because it's an Arab country, but especially for women and teachers it had to be secret. There were only a few Kuwaiti women teaching in schools, it was mainly Palestinians, Egyptians, some Syrians. And my brother and his wife were there too, they were ANM members working in secret also."

Although in its early days in the 1950s the ANM had been a specifically pan-Arab, nationalist organization, in 1960 the group's newspaper published an article which laid out the need not only for struggle on the "political national question" but also to address "an overall revolutionary concept which is the melting-pot of the national, political, economic, and social ambitions of the progressive Arab masses."[45] But this new strand within the ANM was not supported by all, including senior members of the leadership. The leftist trend was strengthened by two influences: the blow to pan-Arab ideas arising from the collapse of the United Arab Republic of Egypt and Syria in 1961, which weakened the position of the pan-Arabists within the ANM; and internal changes made in 1962 when ANM leader George Habash was in prison in Syria. In 1964, a meeting of the ANM's Executive Committee and other senior members debated the Movement's "ideological crisis." This led to changes in the structure of the Movement, granting the national sections more autonomy. Some of these went on to merge with local Nasserite forces or other nationalist movements, as in Iraq, Syria, and Egypt, whilst others remained independent, as in Palestine and parts of the Gulf. This shift allowed the formation of a separate Palestine-interest section and the ultimate development of the PFLP, but it also effectively resulted in the fragmentation of the Arab Nationalist Movement as a single organization.[46] According to a former ANM member, Abd al-Karim Hamad, another fateful decision made in 1964 was the failure of negotiations between the ANM and Fatah over coordinated action. The ANM assented in principle—if a common political program could be agreed on. "Yasser Arafat then said it was not worth the bother," Hamad claims.[47]

From the 1950s onwards the ANM had antagonized many Arab states with its pan-Arab politics and its Nasserite and increasingly socialist views, which especially alarmed the conservative monarchies of the Gulf. In 1966 the ANM also suffered a series of setbacks across the region, with various members of its leadership and cadres jailed and internal divisions hampering its operations. Khaled's brother and other ANM members working in Kuwait were exposed, sacked and deported from the country.[48]

Occasional information about the growth of the Palestinian resistance movement and its developing relationship with figures like Nasser were slowly filtering through to Kuwait, as was news of the Vietnam War, the invasion of the Dominican Republic and, to a broken-hearted Khaled, the assassination of Che Guevara. Khaled herself had from the mid 1960s followed the increasingly left-leaning ANM along the path of socialism. She says that "I couldn't do anything political in Kuwait. I had to be silent because my brother had to leave and who else will provide for the family? So in 1967 the PFLP was founded but I was in Kuwait and I was waiting to hear from anybody but nobody contacted me and I couldn't leave Kuwait." The death of Khaled's father in 1966 further increased the family's dependence on Leila's remittances.

The nascent Popular Front for the Liberation of Palestine separated from its roots in the Arab Nationalist Movement for a number of reasons. The ANM's structure consisted of increasingly autonomous "regional commands" in each country and in 1964, with the new, politically conservative PLO presenting itself as the voice of the Palestinian people, a "Palestine Regional Command" was set up under George Habash to retain the allegiance of ANM supporters in the Palestinian refugee camps of Lebanon and Syria.

According to some histories of the Movement, this regional command morphed into the National Front for the Liberation of Palestine (NFLP), one of the groups which in 1967 would merge to form the PFLP. In November 1964 it acquired its first martyr when a member of a reconnaissance party from its better-known military wing, the Youth of Vengeance, was killed by Israeli forces after crossing the Lebanese border into Northern Israel on a reconnaissance mission.[49] But by the late 1960s, internal tensions and external influences on the ANM had effectively split it into a number of distinct national or regional bodies. In addition, the failure of the Arab regimes to act on their professions of support for the Palestinians, and indeed the

suppression by the Jordanian monarchy of Palestinian attempts
to organize independently, had disillusioned many. As Rayyes
and Nahas wrote in 1976:

> The demonstrable frailty of pan-Arab unity on a practical political level
> convinced those Palestinian activists who had seen the path to liberation
> along Nasserite lines (of an Arab nation in arms against Israel) that they
> could not wait until the rest of the Arab world pulled itself together.
> Now they began to think of liberation through independent Palestinian
> action and an independent Palestinian entity. As a result, more than 30
> Palestinian organizations sprang up (most of which had only a small
> membership).[50]

Although other writers have highlighted divisions in ANM
leadership, Leila Khaled herself puts the split mainly down to
a changing strategy in the movement, recognizing the different
conditions—both on the ground and for political activists—
in each Arab country, and the need for a more decentralized
structure to account for this. "After the defeat in 1967 the
decision was taken that the Palestinians should establish
something else, because the challenges are different, so the PFLP
was established with other militant groups," she says. Khaled
also disputes the involvement of the NFLP in the development
of the Popular Front, although she was not involved in the
armed struggle at the time when other writers describe them
as being active. The question marks over the exact course of
events is not unusual: as one writer put it in the late 1980s,
Palestinian and other Middle Eastern militant organizations tend
to "discourage scholarly interest ... there does not today exist a
single scholarly, or even serious journalistic, work on the PFLP.
The only sources that have touched upon the subject have been
books on 'international terrorism' which very often contain false
and misleading information."[51]

For a short time, Khaled had campaigned for PLO branches
to be set up in Kuwait[52]—despite her later condemnation of
the "upper-class" tendencies of Shukairy and the rest of the
organization's leadership—and in 1967–68 she worked with the
local branch of Fatah, the only Palestinian resistance organization

tolerated in the emirate. At one point, she even asked to be allowed to join its armed wing, Al-Assifa.[53] Formed in the late 1950s by students and other activists, mainly living in the Gulf states and Cairo, Fatah shied away from the left-wing orientation of the ANM and later Palestinian movements, focusing its aim entirely on liberating Palestine through military struggle. The organization had launched itself on January 1, 1965 with an act of sabotage on an Israeli water pipeline, and later the same year revealed that its leader—or spokesman, as he was initially described—was Yasser Arafat.[54]

Like many leftists, however, Khaled was unhappy with Fatah's acceptance of money from sources such as the Saudi regime, which they condemned as reactionary, and skeptical of its lack of a clear political position and strategy, so she was waiting to hear more about the PFLP, of which she had heard rumors.[55] Finally she found a bookstore in Kuwait City selling PFLP cards and made contact with local organizers, undergoing further strategic and ideological training on the road to forming a proper revolutionary cell. News of other PFLP "external operations" in Europe was too much for Khaled to take: she wanted to be a part of them too.[56] But, she says, "I waited until 1968 to go back to Lebanon to find out how I should act and I met Dr Wadi'a Haddad and he told me I had to go back to Kuwait to organize people and start work there again, and to mobilize people for the struggle." Raring to train as a fighter and join the armed struggle, it wasn't what Khaled wanted to hear. But she obeyed, hoping to prove herself worthy of military training by recruiting new members to the Popular Front.

2

Leila the Fighter

The PFLP was formally established at the end of 1967. The Six Day War had signaled the demise of the ANM's initial strategy of trying to provoke conflict between a united Arab world and Israel,[1] and it merged with two other Palestinian organizations, the Heroes of Return and Ahmed Jibril's Palestine Liberation Front. In its early days the organization was, like the ANM, beset by internal conflicts. Nayef Hawatmeh, one of the figures with whom George Habash had regularly clashed in the ANM, left the PFLP in 1969 to form the Popular Democratic Front for the Liberation of Palestine (it later dropped the "Popular" and became the DFLP). Ahmed Jibril also left the PFLP in 1970, objecting to its Marxist politics, and, allegedly, to its insufficiently militaristic outlook,[2] and formed the PFLP-General Command, which carried out major attacks during the 1970s and 1980s.[3]

But despite early splits and setbacks, the PFLP, along with Fatah and smaller Palestinian revolutionary groups such as the Saika, represented in 1967 a new way of "doing" Palestinian politics. They drew on their own experiences as fedayeen (freedom fighters, literally "those who sacrifice [themselves]"). Other influences included the guerrilla writings of Che and Castro, but also the ideas of Frantz Fanon, who emphasized the power of armed, violent action to resurrect the pride and dignity of colonized peoples, and the need for those peoples—like Fanon's own adopted nation of Algeria—to take their struggle into their own hands.[4]

Since 1948, action aimed at regaining rights for the Palestinian people had either been confined to legal measures and lobbying, or framed as part of a larger pan-Arab struggle, which during the 1950s did include armed fedayeen raids across the Jordanian and Egyptian borders but where Palestinian freedom per se often took second place on the political agenda. Some paid lip service to the idea of Palestinian independence whilst harboring designs on their territories or on control of their movements. The leaders of the Arab states, who had failed to provide proper support in 1948, were seen as using the issue of Palestine as a political platform on which they could posture to one another and distract possible dissenters within their own states, without the prospect of any real commitment, political or military.[5] Khaled bitterly recorded in 1973 that nine years earlier, "the honourable presidents and noble kings, without consulting the Palestinian people or considering other candidates, appointed Ahmed Shukairy chairman of the PLO. Shukairy was their man. He could be relied upon to make the necessary flamboyant pronouncements to appease the Palestinian masses, without precipitating a crisis or organising the Palestinians into a fighting force."[6]

Horrified by the Arab armies' resounding defeat by Israel in 1967, Khaled was adamant that she would train as a fighter with the newly formed PFLP. Initially she was told by the organization to be patient: if she could recruit ten new members in a year, she could go to the training camps. She recruited 20 members in just ten months, she says.[7] She also faced opposition from her family, understandably as she was one of the main breadwinners. Her mother wanted her to return to Kuwait, where she could earn a respectable living and send money back to support her younger siblings. "Let your brothers go and be fighters," she was told. But she refused, and took two of her brothers to train with her.

Finally allowed to undergo the military training she had dreamed of, Khaled travelled to a camp north of Amman. There, she learned how to use guns and hand grenades, studied military tactics and trained in hand-to-hand combat. Leila Khaled was fully in her element. She met one of her heroines, Rashida Obeida, who had been an underground PFLP commando and "knew how to handle a gun."[8] "The camp was in the mountains and the training was hard," she told Eileen MacDonald. "It was very cold, even in summertime, and we were living in tents spread over the mountainside. I did not notice the hardships; I was so happy that at last my dream to become a fighter had come true. I was so happy that for the first three days and nights I could not sleep." As well as fellow PFLP recruits, she was training alongside other Palestinian factions and international militants. Understandably, this hotbed of radicalism was being hunted and throughout the summer the camp was moved from one site to another as it was bombed by Israeli airplanes. But Khaled stayed.[9]

Khaled's persistence stood her in good stead. Having completed her basic military instruction she was selected for special training, and finally one day she was called. "The section for outside operations was run by Dr Wadi'a Haddad, and one day they sent me to see him in Lebanon. I was nominated by the chief of the training camp, because he knew how I acted, and because I was already known to Dr Haddad." Despite her assurance after the fact, at the time she had barely believed that she might have been selected; even when she was given weapons to transport back to Beirut, she was convinced that this was all a ploy to get her back to her mother.

Arriving in Beirut, she was asked: "Are you ready to go to prison, to be tortured and not break, to die?"[10] She responded in the affirmative, and was sent to say goodbye to her family, telling them that she was returning to Kuwait.[11] But the following day, as she told Eileen MacDonald in 1991, she nearly lost the mission she had hoped so much for after she got the giggles. "I had this picture in my mind of me carrying a plane on my back and everyone running up to me and trying to take it off," she said. Hijacking was not a joke, she was told sternly, and pulled herself together.[12] Then she was sent for yet more training, instructing her in minute details about the plane, a TWA Boeing 707 on the Rome–Athens–Tel Aviv route, which she was being prepared to attack.

Wadi'a Haddad was already known to the Khaled siblings because of their decade of involvement in the ANM, which Haddad had helped George Habash to found in the early 1950s. Now, he and Leila Khaled would work together closely on both this and subsequent missions. "He was very precise, he always saw the details," she says. "He wanted to follow everything up, all the little things that you cannot control."

Hijacking aircraft, a tactic which for the Western press of the 1970s would become synonymous with the Palestinian resistance, was still a fairly new practice in 1969. Palestinians didn't come up with the tactic, which was first used by Peruvian revolutionaries as far back as 1931. The inaugural Palestinian hijacking had been directed by Wadi'a Haddad in 1968, when two PFLP commandos ordered an Israeli passenger jet to divert to Algiers airport. The plane and hostages were exchanged for Palestinian prisoners in Israeli jails.

Khaled went on at least one reconnaissance trip to Rome in preparation for her 1969 hijacking. Haddad sent her there to scope out the kind of details she says he always considered in his operations: "I memorized the streets, the bus stop, the buildings where I would be that afternoon. Every little detail," she describes. "But when I bought some clothes he said no, this is not suitable, go and buy something else. Even these details. When he thought about a big action like that, he didn't think of it only as one package, he thought of all the details, how to maneuver, how to pass through every door." Eventually, Khaled found a white trouser suit which met with Haddad's approval. The ensemble include a white hat which, despite her insistence that she wasn't interested in clothes, Khaled admitted to loving. "I made a ribbon for it so that if it was pushed off during the hijack I would not lose it," she told Eileen MacDonald.[13]

Setting off on the actual mission, Leila Khaled flew alone from Beirut to Rome, telling the friendly American who tried to engage her in conversation on the plane that she was travelling to meet her fiancé. She spent two days walking around Rome, on her own, but impervious to the historical sights. She was too busy reciting the details of her coming operation to herself.

Khaled only met her companion on the mission, a fellow PFLP commando called Salim Issawi, a short time before the hijacking was to take place. He was a Palestinian, also from Haifa but raised in Syria.[14] "He had been a fighter in a base in Lebanon, near the border, working with other fighters," says Khaled. "He was prepared to do this work first, before he trained for this mission. He was a very solid person, very tall."

Khaled and Issawi had booked seats in first class, picked to put them near to the plane's cockpit. But they didn't pose as a couple, so the attractive Khaled, in her couture clothes, acquired an admirer, a man she described in her 1973 autobiography as Greek-American—from Chicago—and in her later interview with Eileen MacDonald as a "very jolly" Greek who tried to chat her up in the departure lounge. She was reassured by his guesses that she was Latin American or Mediterranean, suggesting that her disguise as an international tourist was working. But he also pricked her conscience, telling her that he was on his way back to Greece after working for 15 years in the USA, and that he hadn't seen his mother in all that time. As Khaled describes the encounter to MacDonald, "I was shocked. I was about to tell him to go away and catch another plane. I remembered my father going to Jerusalem in 1964 to meet his mother. He was given permission to meet her at the [Mandelbaum] Gate and he waited three days but she didn't come. She came the day after he left in despair. She never even heard about his death. I knew very well what it meant to be away from home, from your mother and sisters...." After the hijack, she "approached him as he sat crying and told him, 'Now you are OK. We will send your mother a telegram and she can meet you.'"[15] Khaled denied press reports that she and Issawi had targeted the plane because Israeli general Yitzhak Rabin was supposed to be on board. But other passengers, as described in her 1973 account, included two elderly women and two small girls, one of them wearing a "Make Friends" badge which, again, almost melted Khaled's resolve.[16]

But Leila Khaled hardened her heart and boarded the plane. Sitting opposite Issawi, she accepted a coffee and he a beer, but then tried to fend off further offers of refreshments. Finally, Khaled told the air hostess that she was cold and had a stomach ache and was given an extra blanket, which she used to arrange her hand grenade and pistol where she could reach them easily. Taking advantage of the crew's distraction as they started to serve meals, Salim leaped forward to the cockpit, telling its inhabitants to "listen to their new pilot." He told the crew and passengers that their new captain was "Shadiah Abu Ghazaleh," the name of a PFLP activist, the organization's first female martyr, who had been killed whilst making grenades for the armed struggle.[17] Khaled, meanwhile, uncovered the grenades in her lap and followed him, causing one of the stewards to drop her tray and scream. The move wasn't exactly flawless—Khaled had to wrestle with her pistol, which had slipped down through her loose waistband. Wanting to remain alert, she hadn't eaten that day and the nervous exhilaration of finally carrying out her mission made her laugh as she shook the gun out through the ankle of her trousers.[18] She and Issawi ordered the crew and the first-class passengers to head back into economy so that they couldn't see what was going on at the front of the plane. "But I didn't hear anybody screaming or anything like that," she claims.

Uppermost in Khaled's mind was, she says, "to achieve my mission perfectly."[19] Her role was to communicate with the pilot and air traffic control, to manage the situation on board the plane—in short, to carry out most of the hijacking itself. She aimed to keep the passengers and crew out of the way, "the staff were acting calmly because I invited them to give the people food and anything they needed and they did that. Of course people reacted, it was panic, I'm sure, but I didn't hear anyone shouting or screaming," she repeats. Khaled also delivered political speeches to the passengers, which a female steward translated into French, telling the hijackers that many of the passengers spoke no English and had not understood their instructions to remain calm and seated, or indeed their revolutionary statements.[20] Issawi, meanwhile, was an explosives expert, primarily involved to blow up the plane after it was on the ground and empty.

Initially Khaled directed the pilot to head towards Lod, now Ben Gurion, airport, Israel's main air entry point, built over the birthplace of PFLP founder and first General Secretary George Habash. At one point the engineer tried to trick her by claiming that there was insufficient fuel to fly that far, but with the technical training she had been put through, and Wadi'a Haddad's obsession with detail, she spotted the ploy and got angry. Inside Israeli airspace, the Israeli military scrambled three Mirage fighter jets and flew them close to the hijacked plane which, Khaled claims, panicked the passengers more than the initial takeover—although this might have had more to do with her telling them that they were in more danger from the Israeli jets than from her and her comrade. Khaled was communicating directly with Lod's air traffic control and, says Eileen MacDonald, apparently derived considerable pleasure from forcing them to address her not as Flight TWA 840 but as Flight PFLP Free Arab Palestine. They had initially refused to do so, but complied after the terrified co-pilot shouted at them to do as they were told, because there was a grenade in the cockpit.[21] According to the notes Khaled made in Syrian custody after the hijacking, the Israelis feared that she planned to explode the plane at Lod or over Israeli territory.[22]

Despite the incidents with the Israeli jets and the Lod control tower, and the "fear and hatred" she sensed from the co-pilot, who she told to face away from her because she didn't want to see the look in his eyes, Khaled's overall memories of the hijacking seem to be remarkably uneventful. "I was very calm. Even the pilot spoke about it at his press conference," she claims. "It went smoothly for four hours. I was speaking to the passengers, calming them, telling them our story. I told them, we know that you are not part of this, it will be OK for you. We were forced to do this but you will go back to your countries. So maybe this cooled them down for a while."

The instruction to head for Lod was, however, a bluff, and after passing over the airport to see the Israeli tanks and troops lined up there to deal with them, Khaled ordered the plane to head to Damascus. On the way, however, she told the pilot to make a detour, flying low over her birthplace of Haifa. It is when she describes seeing Haifa from the airplane cockpit that Leila Khaled really comes alive. "It's very clear to me," she says, "these are things that are different from everything else that happens in life." In 1973 she wrote that "My father's image appeared before my eyes and I could hear his voice saying, When shall we return home? My whole world came together."[23] Even in 2008, her eyes widen and she talks with a new animation: "Whenever I'm asked this question, I can't say the words, I can't say the real things that I felt at that moment. When we flew over Tel Aviv, the first moment that I saw Palestine, I forgot that I was doing an operation, I forgot it totally. I just wanted to see it with my eyes. And then when I saw Haifa ... whenever I remember it, my house, a little bit of me is lost there, it was like I was practicing my alphabet. It was a very passionate moment. I just wanted to call my grandmother, my aunts, everybody who was still there and tell them that we are coming back. Even the pilot, when he was in the press conference, said 'I felt how passionate she was, I even saw the hairs on her face standing up...' Because I was standing over him and he was looking at me."

The plight of the terrified passengers on hijacked airplanes is, of course, the issue often forgotten by those who idolize fighters like Leila Khaled. Civilian travelers going about their daily business become pawns in affairs often well outside their knowledge. "We were instructed that you don't hurt anyone," insists Khaled. "The first thing is, you are not there to kill anyone, those people have nothing to do with this conflict. Second, you have to apologize to them, and treat the crew lightly. I was the one who was terrified. I had to speak to them, to speak to the air traffic control stations. Salim was just sitting there, his role was to protect me."

Leila Khaled is perhaps being disingenuous here. The PFLP—and Khaled herself—justified airplane hijackings as a temporary tactic to bring the plight of the Palestinian people to world attention, to shift international perspectives on them from hazy awareness of a pitiful refugee population to understanding that this was an issue of land, politics, national liberation, and the displacement of an entire people with the collusion of the Western powers. As Khalil Meqdisi, a modern-day PFLP spokesman, puts it: "Outside of Palestine and the Arab world, the Palestinian question was not visible. Palestinian fighters were dying in their operations and Palestinians were subjected to all kinds of massacres and oppression by the Israeli occupation but the world turned a blind eye and at the state and media level they didn't want to address the Palestinian question." Airplane hijackings were the grand theatrical stunts which would attract this attention, open up the debate, and generate this new international understanding of the situation.

In a post-9/11 world it is hard to grasp the extent to which the meaning of hijackings and the reactions of hijacked passengers have changed. David Raab, a teenage passenger on one of the planes hijacked by Khaled's comrades a year later, recorded in his diary at the time that: "The first feeling—at least on my part— was one of excitement. I had been reading about hijackings for the past couple of years, and I figured it always happened to the other guy. It never happened to you. And here I was, sitting in the middle of one of those hijackings. So—not knowing who had hijacked us or for what purpose—I just had a feeling of excitement at first."[24] No one would have this response now; in fact, there is an argument that hijacking is now largely a defunct tactic. Today, with the Twin Towers the archetype of an airplane hijacking in most people's minds, the assumption has to be that to be hijacked means to die—and therefore passengers have nothing to lose by challenging their attackers.

But in 1969, hijackings were a relatively new occurrence, and passengers on hijacked craft were for the main part delivered, shaken but unharmed, to their embassies. They had no reason to assume that they would die. Nevertheless, hijacking is by definition a tactic which relies on fear—of injury to passengers or airplane crew, fear that the pilot will panic or be injured or have a heart attack and the plane will crash. Or that ransom or political demands made by the hijackers will not be met and they will commit further violence to up the ante. Or that one of the grenades being waved around will go off by accident, blowing a hole in the fuselage. However many apologies are issued—or, as David Raab notes in his account of events in 1970, however much free whiskey is distributed around the plane[25]—hijackings are still dependent on the terror of the passengers and crew to work. There are too many victims in this picture: the Jewish communities suffering centuries of European anti-Semitic persecution in which the Palestinians played no part; the Palestinian people massacred and expelled from their land to assuage Western Holocaust guilt; the passengers and crew of a civilian aircraft terrified by two people with hand grenades and guns. Each can put forward an argument for why they are entitled to impose their will on the less powerful link in the chain.

Many supporters of the Palestinian cause, especially those who
see Leila Khaled as a glamorous heroine, believe that the end of
drawing global attention to the plight of the Palestinians justifies
the means of hijacking.

Khaled says that hijacking was "a tactic not a strategy. After
the last PFLP hijackings we concentrated on operations in
Occupied Palestine and on defending ourselves in Lebanon,
against the Lebanese army and the Israelis." And, she insists,
impassioned and at times tearful, as a tactic it was both justified
and effective: "In all my time, in all my statements, I always said
we were forced to do it. It wasn't because we liked to do it, we
knew beforehand that those people, the passengers, had nothing
to do with the conflict. But before, nobody heard our screaming
from the tents. Nobody wanted to hear or listen or learn about
our sufferings. Nobody heard those who were tortured in jails.
Or even if they knew they don't want to do anything about it.
So we couldn't see other ways, and we just used it for a short
time, just to ring the bell in this world. We felt that there was
injustice against us and nobody wanted to hear that. In fact, no
one was killed or injured in the PFLP's hijackings except some
of the militants. It was a panic for people for a short time, but
we never meant to hurt anyone. For our people there had been
years and years of suffering, under occupation or in the diaspora,
and yet no one wanted to show this side of things."

On touchdown at Damascus airport, which the PFLP regarded
as friendly soil, Salim Issawi got to perform his main task; he
wired explosives into the cockpit of the TWA plane and, after
several false starts, blew it off, leaving the rest of the fuselage
standing on the tarmac, "like a fish with its head chopped off," in
the words of one newspaper.[26] They had, they believed, succeeded
in their primary objective—to bring the plight of the Palestinian
people to the world's attention. Khaled and Issawi were then,
to the horror of the passengers who had just fled the hijacked
plane at a run, loaded onto the airport bus with them. Scared,
in shock—some of them had wet themselves—the last thing
they wanted was to be accompanied by their hijackers to the
airport building. And, says Eileen MacDonald of her interview
with Khaled in 1991, the hijacker was apparently surprised to

have met with fear and hostility from some of her captives, who refused the sweets and cigarettes she had handed round the bus from the same handbag she had carried her grenades in. But, says MacDonald, Khaled found vindication in one encounter on the bus. A woman passenger "sighed and shook her head. 'I don't understand. Who are the Palestinians?' she asked."[27]

"We were questioned first at the airport," says Khaled, "and then we were taken to the offices of one of the security apparatuses and put underground, each one in our own cell. These were in different places and we didn't know where the other was." The initial questioning was hostile, with a soldier telling Khaled that "this action is not fedayeen-like. It is terrorism."[28] The Syrians' attitude had relaxed by the following morning. "The next day they called me and I was met by about 20 officers in a room with a table. I was on one side of the table and the main officer was on the other and they were speaking to me, not like they were interrogating a criminal but as if they just wanted to discuss it. Afterwards I thought that it was if they appreciated what I had done but they had to do it. But I was very nervous about it, I wanted to know 'why are you asking me'?"

According to some sources, the Syrians' initial reaction was fury, assuming that Khaled and Issawi were Egyptian intelligence agents seeking to attack Syria as part of the hostility which had developed after the disintegration of the United Arab Republic in 1961. When it emerged that they were, in fact, from the PFLP, they were treated—as Khaled describes—more like naughty but indulged children. They were told off for "embarrassing" Syria and for putting it under international pressure to extradite commandos who Syria, in theory, supported.

Khaled and Issawi were held for a week until they went on hunger strike, something they repeated several times over the next six weeks. On one occasion, after a week refusing food, Khaled fainted and woke up in hospital, on a drip but with visitors—her mother and sisters. Despite her opposition to Khaled training as a PFLP fighter, Khaled's mother told the press that she was proud of her daughter. But Khaled was told that she and Issawi would be held while negotiations over the Israeli passengers from the plane were completed. Also, Khaled claims, the Syrian authorities told her that they couldn't be seen to condone her activities and had to hold her, "but this wasn't convincing to me." Two Israeli women passengers had already been freed, but the Syrians, still technically at war with Israel, claimed that there were still issues over two Israeli males. The Israelis had been separated from the rest of the passengers as soon as they were identified by the Syrian authorities at Damascus.[29] Eventually, the final two hostages were released in exchange for two Syrian air force pilots who were being held by the Israelis, and several imprisoned fedayeen.[30] And finally, after six weeks first in police cells and then under house arrest, Khaled and Issawi were also allowed to go.

Hijackings carried out by Palestinian groups in the late 1960s and early 1970s certainly meant that few people in the USA and Europe could continue to claim to have no idea who the Palestinians were. But the extent to which this new knowledge had a positive impact is questionable. To movement members like Leila Khaled hijackings brought the Palestinian people to the world's attention, and it is true that a few people had their interest sparked enough to read further, to acquire books like Khaled's own 1973 autobiography, and to set these terrifying and disruptive acts into some kind of wider political context. But for many, it simply turned Palestinians from a group of people they had never heard of into a group of people they associated irrevocably with the word "terrorist." As anthropologist Rosemary Sayigh put it in her 1979 book *The Palestinians: From Peasants to Revolutionaries:*

the rise of Resistance Movement after 1967 gave birth to a new stereotype: instead of refugees, Palestinians now became terrorists. Few newspaper readers remembered that Palestinians were themselves the victims of terrorism. Few could imagine the conditions (political and material) out of which the Resistance rose. Even fewer rejected the false distinction between state terrorism ("military action") and revolutionary terrorism. Palestinian violence was, and continues to be, condemned by the same media that draw a veil over the past of men like Begin, Allon or Lahis [Israeli politicians involved in the 1948 war and in the cases of Begin and Lahis accused of direct involvement in massacres such as Deir Yassin].[31]

For Lina Makboul, a film director of Palestinian origin who says she hero-worshipped Leila Khaled as a teenager, her film *Leila Khaled: Hijacker* was in part a quest to find out how Khaled feels about the idea that she might have been substantially responsible for the terrorist stereotyping that Makboul and many other Palestinians have faced, and for the suffering which thousands of ordinary Palestinians experienced in events such as Black September in Jordan in 1970, when the Jordanian army drove the Palestinian resistance out of the country.

But at the time, hijackings rarely resulted in casualties, and for the Western media, fascinated by novelty, the "girl hijacker" was a big part of the story. Even before she was released, press coverage of the incident quoted passengers talking about "a young, very beautiful and attractive girl ... she was elegantly dressed" and in one case referring to Khaled as a "chick."[32] According to Khaled, her appearance was even a topic for discussion at the pilot's press conference after the hijacking. "He was saying she's beautiful, very attractive," she says. "My sisters were telling my mother, this is Leila, because no photos had come out yet and she was saying, 'I know my daughter, bring me the photos, she's not like they are saying, all this beauty and so on.' And they were making jokes about it. Later on, it was not the PFLP who released the first photos of me. One of the teachers I worked with in Kuwait, when she heard the name they had from the plane's manifest, she gave the media the pictures."

Leila Khaled apparently did not anticipate the storm of attention she would be stepping into once she left Syrian custody. She is often credited with being the first female hijacker, though some sources suggest that she was beaten by three years—that one of a group calling themselves the Condors, who hijacked a plane to the Falkland Islands in 1966 to claim them for Argentina, was a woman.[33] She wasn't the first female PFLP commando to undertake a high-profile international operation: Amina Dhahbour had been part of a unit which attacked an El Al plane at Zurich airport in February 1968, killing three passengers and a pilot.[34] But she was certainly the first young, attractive, outspoken Audrey Hepburn-lookalike to appear in Reuters images clutching a Kalashnikov in front of an airplane (although these photos were, according to Khaled, taken in Lebanon well after the fact).

Indeed, some of the initial effects of the publicity were negative. Khaled returned from Syria to Lebanon to visit her family, and found that her brother Walid had been beaten up by the Lebanese gendarmerie once her name came out.[35] The PFLP hadn't made proper plans to deal with the impact of widespread attention. According to Khaled, "it was not meant that I would be exposed. We as the Popular Front didn't want to expose me to the media. It was a new era and we didn't think of the media as a means for the struggle. There were no satellites, internet, you know, everything was local. We depended more on the radio than TV."

If this was indeed the case, and Khaled "the hijack girl" was only exposed to the glare of publicity via the snapshot of a former colleague, the PFLP seem to have rapidly adapted to the situation. According to MacDonald,

> the PFLP leadership were delighted with the publicity and sent their star comrade on an extensive tour of the Middle East. They supplied her with her own retinue of bodyguards, well aware that she was at the top of the list for kidnap or assassination by the Israelis. To the Arab world, she was a heroic figure: students at AUB mobbed her, parties and dinners were held in her honour. A British businessman who was introduced to her at an Embassy party in Qatar commented, "she was fêted like a visiting astronaut."[36]

Khaled's version of the tour was less glamorous: "I was on a three-month tour of the Arab Gulf and Iraq with a team of revolutionary stalwarts ... the purpose of the tour was to spread revolutionary propaganda. We not only reached out and communicated with the Arab masses, but learned a good deal about their concerns, especially their desire to oust the British from the Arab Gulf."[37] Other commentators note that the PFLP apparently received a large donation from the Abu Dhabi royal family in the wake of the tour.[38]

Khaled still seems ambivalent about her first media experiences. "We learnt from that that we shouldn't expose everybody, that it's enough for one person to do this and that's it," she says, decisively and a little grimly. And after her second, even more spectacular, hijacking, even the other female commandos who took part remained anonymous—partly, says Khaled, because one was from the Occupied Territories and had to be protected from retribution by the Israeli authorities, and partly because "it was intended like that by the PFLP, no more exposing people."

Members of the Popular Front for the Liberation of Palestine (PFLP) drinking tea during a training excercise, circa 1969. Among the group are Leila Khaled (centre, left) and Salim Issawi (centre, right). (Popperfoto / Getty Images)

After several months of celebrity, Khaled also apparently realized that being so highly recognizable could affect her future freedom to act as she wished. She wanted to return quietly to her revolutionary work in Wahdat camp in Amman, where the PFLP was still based. The PFLP leadership were not, however, particularly sympathetic to her new-found shyness, she says:

"A group of Italian TV came to Jordan, to the house where I was staying. I opened the door and they said, 'where is Leila

Khaled?' I said she wasn't here and maybe she was in the camp and they went to the camp and said, she's not here. So they left and went back to Beirut. But Dr George Habash was very angry and he called me and said they wanted to meet me. I said I didn't want to, and he asked why. I said I was afraid, I don't want to speak to them. I was crying. But he said you have to go out to them, so I washed my face and went out. The camera team was shocked, they asked why I did it. I said I was afraid and they said, 'what, you frightened the whole world and you are afraid of us?' I said yes, I'm tired, I don't want to answer any questions and they laughed at that, and everyone was laughing..."

What Leila couldn't say, even to George Habash, was that Wadi'a Haddad had already promised her another high-profile mission. She had realized that her increasingly well-known face could jeopardize that. Despite the PFLP's new taste for the publicity that their celebrated hijacker had generated, Khaled herself cared, she says, more about being a commando than a celebrity.

3
Black September

Leila Khaled returned to her base in Jordan, where by the spring of 1970 sporadic outbreaks of fighting between the Hashemite monarchy's troops and the Palestinian fighters were already the norm. Relations between Palestinian and Arab nationalist organizations and the Jordanian monarchy had been tense since the early 1960s, before the establishment of the PLO.[1] King Hussein and politicians such as Prime Minister Wasfi Tal firmly maintained that the West Bank, administered by Jordan between 1948 and 1967, would remain Jordanian territory, and that the futures of the Jordanian and Palestinian peoples were irrevocably linked—under Hashemite leadership.[2] At various points during the 1960s the Jordanian authorities closed down Fatah and PLO offices in Jerusalem and Amman.[3] They banned organizations such as the General Union of Palestinian Women (GUPW) after its members took part in protests against the Jordanians' refusal to allow West Bank villages near the border with Israel to fortify themselves, leaving them vulnerable to attacks like that on Samu', a town near Hebron, in 1966.[4] The growing frequency of fedayeen raids over the border into Israel worsened this situation, as the Hashemite regime struggled to balance the need to be seen to support the Palestinian cause in front of other Arab regimes, whilst avoiding Israeli reprisals for the resistance's activities. And as the resistance organizations grew stronger and more confident, they operated freely in substantial areas of Amman and towns such as Irbid in the north, challenging King Hussein's authority and, in the case of the PFLP, openly calling for an end to "reactionary" monarchies such as that of the Hashemites.[5]

In November 1968 the cat-and-mouse game of legal restrictions and police suppression of Palestinian organizations came to a head with "clashes in Amman [which] left 24 dead and

89 injured." The regime tried to impose curfews and there were rounds of arrests, but the fedayeen still controlled major roads out of the Jordanian capital and acted unchecked in many parts of the country.[6] Wahdat camp was known as the "Republic of Palestine" and was home to the PFLP's Jordanian HQ,[7] but in other camps and parts of Amman King Hussein's "goons" and local security forces prevented Khaled from delivering some of the post-hijack lectures she had been assigned in 1969 and early 1970.[8] According to contemporary accounts, by 1970 armed encounters between the Palestinian resistance and the Jordanian army were daily events, and Leila Khaled took part in them. So did some other women guerrillas, including Leila's comrade Nadia, who led a squad in raids on Jordanian police stations to capture weapons,[9] and Fatah's Um Nasser, who described how

> There were clashes [with the Jordanian forces] near Salt in Jordan and we used to fight. I used to stand guard till morning. There were very difficult times. Sometimes, when I would go to one of our brother fighters and tell him "give me the gun because it is time for my guard duty," he would find it very hard to give it to a sister. Afterwards, they passed beyond that complex and we became part of them.[10]

Despite her role in the grassroots resistance, Khaled desperately wanted to carry out another high-profile mission, and she didn't want her recognizable face to stop her. She couldn't reverse the media attention she'd received since the Rome hijacking. But she could change her face.

The PFLP found a plastic surgeon in Beirut and Khaled told him that she was planning to get married in Europe but was wanted by Interpol, so she needed to make sure she wasn't recognized. The doctor wasn't convinced, but he was also afraid of her reputation and demanded that she sign a statement that he had been threatened if he refused to carry out the operations. After the final round of surgery he told Khaled that he didn't want to see her face any more. "Don't be afraid," she told him. "We can keep our secrets, who did this for me."

Khaled had a total of six operations on her nose, cheeks, eyes and mouth, to alter her appearance and after her second hijacking

The iconic image of Khaled has been adapted by Palestinian solidarity movements around the world: this version is to be found on the Israeli Separation Wall at Bethlehem Checkpoint. The original was taken by Eddie Adams, best known for his 1968 photograph of General Nguyễn Ngọc Loan executing a Vietcong prisoner on a Saigon street.
(Sarah Irving)

to change it back. The change was, she says, substantial. "For those who didn't already know me and who depended on the pictures, they wouldn't have known me. For someone who knew me before the surgery, they would have recognized me but they would have seen something wrong." The repeated surgery was needed because the first few efforts to change the shape of her nose weren't successful, and even after the final operation, "I looked as if I had an accident," she says. "It was very ugly, but it was what I wanted—the Israeli officer in Amsterdam didn't know me." For decades after, Khaled suffered headaches which had started with the first round of surgery on her nose.[11]

Even before the hijacking of TWA 840 in 1969, Khaled says, Wadi'a Haddad had told her that if she carried out her first mission successfully she would be sent on another, although he hadn't specified what it would be. On trips from Jordan to Lebanon the two of them started preparations for another hijacking, working from Haddad's apartment which, says Khaled, was like a "beehive," with every room filled with people having meetings and making plans.

By this time the Israeli military was viewing PFLP leaders and high-profile figures such as Khaled as targets ripe for attack. One night in May 1970, as the pair were working on their plans at Wadi'a Haddad's home in Beirut, the house was struck by six rockets. "We had already prepared for one operation," says Khaled, "and I had to leave at six in the morning. It was already two in the morning and I was writing some notes about the operation for the morning, to be sent to the leadership in Jordan. I told him, look, I feel sleepy and I have to travel, I need clips to keep my eyes open, I can't go on like this. We had been working since morning but he was such a dynamic person, he worked 13, 15 hours a day continuously. Sometimes he forgot to eat and if you're working with him and you want to stop and eat, he would say 'there are people in prison and they are not given food.' You felt from his personality that this was somehow a person of importance. It was the same with George Habash, but the difference was that you felt that George Habash was the brains and Wadi'a Haddad was the one who translated the thoughts into action. I think even while he slept he was thinking about how to face the enemy. He tried to teach us to be like him, but we couldn't. One of the women comrades was on an operation, she had to leave at 5 a.m. to go to the airport and she hadn't slept. She asked me, is he always like that? He had told her, you can sleep on the plane."

As Khaled begged to be allowed to sleep, Haddad told her she could have five minutes. That, however, was the moment that the rockets struck. Khaled and Haddad were unhurt, but his wife and son Hani were both injured. "Hani was bleeding from the chest and his feet looked squashed," Leila wrote several years later.[12] The Lebanese police were, Khaled says, suspicious of what the pair had been doing at the kitchen table at two o'clock in the morning. Typically, she told the police tersely that they had been "sitting."

The plotters didn't give up—in fact, they moved into a room in the hospital where Haddad's wife and child were being treated and drew up yet more elaborate plans, driven not only by Wadi'a Haddad's fierce commitment to freeing Palestinian prisoners through hostage negotiations, but also by a desire for revenge for the rocket attack. "I was thinking how to retaliate," says Khaled. "I found that there were three planes coming from Tel Aviv, through Europe to New York. I told Wadi'a, we could do this, with SwissAir and TWA and so on, and we could release the prisoners in Israeli jails and also in Zurich. And we began to think."

Leila Khaled's role in the plot was kept hidden even from the other commandos taking part, several of whom were women. She was responsible for training them for the operation, but they didn't know that she had chosen—despite arguments with Wadi'a Haddad, who wanted her to take a safer role in the mission—to take the hardest target, an El Al plane.

*   *   *

At the beginning of September 1970, Leila Khaled made her way from Lebanon to Europe. On the 4th, she met Patrick Arguello, code name Rene, for the first time. He was to be her companion on her second hijack operation, and in Stuttgart together they reviewed their plans. He also did not know who she was. On September 6 they caught a flight from Stuttgart to Amsterdam together, with onward tickets to New York.

Arguello was a Nicaraguan, born in the USA and with an American passport, associated with the Sandinista movement. His mother thought that he was studying in Europe. Indeed, when she found out from a Nicaraguan newspaper on September 14 that he had been killed, she had only just received a letter from him.[13] When she visited Europe to recover her son's body his friends showed her pictures from a secret trip he had made in March 1970 to the Palestinian refugee camps in Jordan. The conditions were, she said, "unliveable."[14] It was this, apparently, which inspired him to volunteer with the PFLP. Given his previous political engagement, it seems a more credible story than unsubstantiated rumors that he was a mercenary who had joined the operation for a $5,000 fee.[15]

Khaled and Arguello landed in Amsterdam where they passed through the transit lounge to their economy class seats for El Al flight 219, a Boeing 707. They didn't know, as they boarded, that the other two PFLP commandos who were supposed to back them up in the hijacking had been refused seats on the plane—apparently because El Al staff had security concerns about them, although they seem to have failed to pass this on to Pan Am. According to Khaled, "Patrick and I had come as transit passengers, but they came in from Amsterdam and they were told there were no more seats. So they bought tickets on a Pan Am plane." In planning this operation it had been decided that an El Al flight would need more hijackers than most airplanes because El Al carried more security guards and would be a more dangerous target. They also underwent more security checks, including a total of three bag and luggage searches,[16] but by modern standards the aviation security of the day was rudimentary, mainly dependent on hand-searching bags; routine scans for luggage were not introduced until several years later.[17] Then the 11.20 flight Khaled and Arguello were booked onto was delayed. There was no Greek suitor this time, but watching the children who were boarding the flight she was about to attack as they played in the departure lounge did, she says, upset her.

By this time Leila Khaled had undergone several rounds of plastic surgery; when a security guard in the departure lounge asked if she was carrying any weapons she denied it emphatically and asked "why would a girl like me have a pistol or a knife, officer?" Fooled, he said sorry.[18] But when Arguello complained that he was hungry and Khaled told him to hold off, that his senses would be sharper if he didn't eat, he demanded to know what kind of queen she thought she was. She replied that she had had a little experience of hijacking, at which he studied her features, murmuring, "Yes, I remember your face."[19]

Unfortunately for Khaled and particularly Arguello, he was not the only person to whom she seemed familiar. An air marshal several rows back also started staring at her, apparently in recognition. Khaled decided that they had to act before he could alert other crew members, even though the plane was barely out of Dutch airspace and it was earlier in the flight than they had planned.[20]

They were sitting in the economy section, further back than Khaled had done on the TWA flight,[21] and when Khaled ran to the cockpit door the pilot had already locked it and she couldn't get through. She pulled out the non-ferrous hand grenades she had been hiding in a specially constructed bra, but the air marshals started shooting. Patrick fired back to defend her—wounding air marshal Shlomo Vider in the leg[22]—but was himself shot, while a passenger shouted that Khaled herself was carrying a grenade so not to shoot her in case it went off. Instead, she was tackled by two of the guards and two passengers. The men started beating her, breaking several ribs. Meanwhile the ingenious pilot dropped the plane into a steep dive, throwing Khaled off her feet to make her vulnerable but not affecting the passengers and crew, who were mainly strapped in. It also brought the airplane into the lower atmosphere, where even if a grenade did go off the cabin would not de-pressurize and the damage would be more limited.[23]

Khaled, in the chaos, thought that one of her grenades actually had gone off but quickly realized that she was wrong.[24] (David Raab, who decades later wrote a book based on his experience as a hostage on one of the other planes, claimed that these were dummies, but there seems to be no corroborating evidence for this.[25]) She had no time to react, though; as a passenger pulled off her wig and she laughed at him he lashed out with his booted feet, knocking her out. She then claims that, as she came to, she watched an air marshal walk up to a wounded and bleeding Arguello, stand on his hips, and fire four bullets into his back.[26] Other accounts also state that air marshal Moti (Mordechai) Bar-Levav "finished emptying his seven-bullet clip into Arguello and Kol karate-chopped the back of Arguello's neck, apparently breaking it."[27] Arguello's death was ruled to be lawful homicide at an inquest in Uxbridge in October 1970. His mother issued a statement saying: "My husband and I deny that we are ashamed of Pat. We are proud that he felt so deeply about the Palestinians that he was prepared to die for them." The coroner also ruled that there was no evidence to support the claim that he had been shot in the head after being tied up, but that the bullet wounds lay in a line across his body, consistent with being shot in a fire-fight.[28]

Concerned about the condition of Shlomo Vider, the security guard who had been shot, the El Al pilot made an emergency landing at London. He touched down in the UK reluctantly, fearing that his security officers could be snatched and prosecuted for shooting Arguello, and that his living hijacker might be confiscated.[29] But realizing that another El Al flight was due to leave Heathrow, he allowed Bar-Levav, the guard who had shot Arguello, to drop out of the plane's hatch and be snatched up into the other El Al plane as it taxied down the runway, headed out of British jurisdiction.[30] Khaled herself was tied up with the neckties of some of the passengers and had to lie on the floor, dazed and covered in blood, as Israeli security guards and British police fought over her while the plane sat on the tarmac in London. Fortunately for Khaled, this meant that she wasn't taken into Israeli custody, but British. The tug-of-war between the Israelis at her feet and the British hanging onto her arms ended and she was bundled out of the plane and, along with Arguello's body, whisked away in an ambulance.

"I was hoping against hope that Patrick would live," Khaled wrote of that ambulance ride. "In a few minutes a nurse ... took the oxygen mask off Patrick's mouth. I knew he was dead. I pleaded with the British to untie me ... I stood beside Patrick's body: I held his hands; I surveyed his wounds; I touched his smashed head; I kissed his lips in a spirit of camaraderie and love. I wept unashamedly."[31]

At Hillingdon hospital, Khaled was X-rayed and, she recalled, "I remember one of the woman cops in the hospital telling me that the doctor was a Jew. I said I did not mind. 'Are you serious?' she asked. I told her I was against Zionists, not Jews, and this doctor was British not an Israeli. She did not understand the difference and I was in too much pain to explain."[32] And then she was confronted by a British immigration official, demanding to know why she had no visa to enter the country.

Forty years later, Khaled still becomes visibly emotional as she talks about Patrick Arguello's death. According to her autobiography, she continued to write notes to him while she was in British detention.[33] In the way that the mind often latches onto an insignificant detail, she has obviously focused on the fact that she refused to allow him to eat before they carried out their mission, and tears appear in her eyes as she describes her reaction to his death: "The first time they brought me food I began to cry," she says. "I told them I didn't want to see it. On the plane, because we came from a different flight, they had given us boxes with sandwiches and cake. Patrick had said when we got on the El Al flight, I am hungry. I said, no, after half an hour we will eat. So when they brought me the food the next day I was crying because of Patrick, because he died and he was hungry and I didn't let him eat."

"It was very painful for me that he was killed, because I felt it should have been me. In the ambulance I was shouting and screaming and when they told me he had passed away I was talking to him in Arabic, telling him that I should have been the one to be killed, because it was my struggle and he was here to support us. Then I realized that he didn't understand Arabic so I was speaking in English, so the British police in the ambulance could also understand it, and they didn't know who he was."

*   *   *

Far away from London, confusion and panic reigned on the other airlines. The two men who were supposed to back up Khaled and Arguello on the El Al flight had taken the initiative—and their weapons—and hijacked the Pan Am flight they had transferred to. Although El Al had decided not to let them onto its plane, Pan Am ground crew were apparently told that they had simply been "denied boarding," and as the two "nice young men" had "co-operated fully" with searches they were allowed into their first-class seats. Captain Priddy, on the Pan Am flight, later said that if he had known that they hadn't been bumped off the El Al flight because of overcrowding but because of fears about hijackers, he wouldn't have let them on his own plane.[34]

As the two men—Mazen Abu Mehana, a Palestinian originally from Haifa, and Samir Abdel Meguid, from Jerusalem, flying on Senegalese passports under the names Diop and Gueye[35]— settled onto the flight, the captain came over to talk to them. He asked them if they had indeed been planning to fly with El Al and gave both of them a quick body search, which missed the weapons they were carrying. The plane took off just after two o'clock, and at about half past they burst into the cockpit with pistols and a grenade, one of them holding a crew member as a human shield.[36] Confused by their impromptu choice of a new target and without clear instructions, the hijackers weren't sure where to take the plane, so Captain Priddy told his pilot to head for Beirut, in the hope that the women and children, at least, would be released there. Beirut air traffic control wanted nothing to do with the situation and claimed that their main runway was under repair and that the secondary strip couldn't take the weight of the Pan Am jumbo jet. The nervous hijackers, however, had decided that landing in Beirut would allow them to talk to senior PFLP representatives and demanded to head there. After a tense couple of hours on the tarmac at Beirut—made worse by Lod control tower trying to lure the plane to Israel, enraging the hijackers—the plane was refueled and headed to Cairo.

The hijackers received a cryptic message at Beirut, that "in Cairo they will precisely act in like manner as Abu-Doummar [Salim Issawi] and Leila Khaled have acted ... but they have to avoid all the mistakes that occurred in the operation of Leila Khaled and Abu Doummar at Damascus Airport. You remember what happened at Damascus Airport?—the way Abu Doummar and Leila Khaled acted—but they have to avoid the mistakes that occurred. This means that the operation must be accomplished in the perfect manner, the front and the rear, that is, the nose and the tail."[37] This meant that, unlike at Damascus, when only the cockpit of the airplane was blown up and TWA was able to bring it back into service just six weeks later, the whole of the Pan Am plane was to be completely destroyed. After explosives were loaded at Beirut the plane landed at Cairo; the passengers were given only minutes to clear the plane before the two hijackers complied. According to some sources, the choice of Cairo was intended by the PFLP as a message to Nasser not to initiate peace talks with Israel; Khaled believes the PFLP was more concerned that the desert airport could not support a jumbo jet.

According to Leila Khaled, the Scotland Yard detectives questioning her thought that there was something more behind the choice of the Pan Am flight. "They asked, how did you know that the NATO budget was there?" she claims. Confidential NATO budget plans were, apparently, hidden in a secret compartment between the inner and outer walls of the Pan Am aircraft, and the security services thought that the Pan Am flight had deliberately been targeted because of them. But it also seems to have been rapidly figured out that the hijacking of the plane with the NATO papers was a fluke, after the details of the hijackers' conversation with the plane's captain emerged.

Unlike the El Al and Pan Am flights, the other hijackings Wadi'a Haddad had organized for September 6, 1970 had gone according to plan. Swissair Flight 100 from Zurich to New York and TWA Flight 714, heading from Frankfurt to New York, both ended up far from their intended destinations, on a deserted ex-British RAF airstrip in the north-east of Jordan called Dawson's Field. Women commandos had been involved in both hijackings. On September 9, they were joined by a BOAC jet which had taken off from Bahrain and been hijacked by another Palestinian, according to some sources acting alone, although contemporary news reports name a female hijacker, "Muna Abid el-Sajid."[38] The second plane and its hostages were apparently intended as a possible bargaining counter for Leila Khaled's release, although Khaled denies that the PFLP itself was involved in this operation.

Initially the hundreds of hostages were held on the aircraft in baking desert sun and freezing night temperatures. David Raab, a Jewish passenger on the TWA flight, described the female hijacker from his plane as: "31 years old and pretty. She had dark curly hair and was quiet and understated; one crew member called her sweet (the crew would later award her a TWA Wings pin). She told the crew that she was to have been married the day the 6-Day War broke out, that her fiancé had been killed in the war, and that she would marry once the Palestinian-Israeli conflict subsided. She said that she had a sister with children in Cincinnati and relatives imprisoned in Israel because they were affiliated with the PFLP."[39]

Some of the hijackers were, according to accounts from the passengers on the various aircraft, kind and respectful, with one British mother telling the press that "they were very pleasant, extremely helpful and they loved the children, which was something everybody noticed."[40] But others, apparently, were not. Raab states that some of the other commandos were rude, aggressive, and occasionally sexually harassed female hostages— although he also conceded that these men were quickly removed by their ranking officers. Kosher food was rarely available to the hostages and as a result Raab and his mother and siblings often went hungry. He also described a male hostage being taken into the desert and forced to lie in a mock grave with guns pointed at his head, after one of the PFLP guerrillas had decided that he might be hiding electronic equipment.[41]

Many of the hostages, especially women and children, were released as early as September 7 and driven to the Intercontinental Hotel in Amman.[42] But many were not, particularly men and anyone, including women and children, suspected of being Israeli citizens or of having anything to do with the State of Israel. For these hostages, conditions deteriorated, with food becoming more sporadic at times and no power available to drain the stinking airplane toilets. Frantic and often hostile negotiations were going on, involving various parties. These included the PFLP; the countries with hostages (including France, Switzerland, Germany, and the USA), and Britain, which had no hostages on board the first two planes but was holding Leila Khaled, and had a large group of hostages, including several children, on the BOAC flight. Israel was also involved, taking a persistently hard line on the proposed hostage swaps being demanded by the PFLP, along with the Red Cross/Red Crescent, who were at times allowed to check on the hostages, the Jordanian authorities, and other Arab powers, headed by Nasser.

Throughout the next three weeks, hostages were released in small groups, including more women and children and some men who were identified as having no Israeli or American connections. But for many of the hostages, this was a jump from the frying pan into the fire. Tensions had been rising for months between the Hashemite regime in Jordan and the Palestinian resistance organizations. But this vast hostage situation and the international attention that accompanied it were the final straw, and an all-out confrontation between the regime and the Palestinian resistance erupted. It came to be known as "Black September." The Syrian government took the opportunity to send tanks over Jordan's northern border to support the Palestinian forces, and Israel massed its troops on the other side of the upper Jordan River, threatening to join in the melee. At times, it looked as if the entire Middle East could explode into war.

All of the hostages were removed to various sites around the country before the planes were detonated in a spectacular series of desert fireballs on September 12. Held in buildings ranging from the Intercontinental Hotel to hovels in Palestinian refugee camps, they had to endure the events of Black September along with their Palestinian captors. Amazingly, none of the hostages was killed, although thousands of Palestinians and Jordanians were. Indeed Leila Khaled also tells stories of the statements made by some of the hostages, including plane crews, on their return: "one of the captains, when he came to London, he said on the radio, 13 of those men [the PFLP commandos], were killed guarding us, but still they made sure to bring us water and food." George Habash also addressed the hostages who were held at the Intercontinental Hotel, apologizing for having delayed and inconvenienced them, but explaining that the Palestinians had been waiting in miserable conditions for years for the chance to return home. According to Khaled, it was not part of the original plan to blow up the planes, but after coming under attack from the Jordanian army, the PFLP felt it had no other choice.

*   *   *

Leila Khaled, meanwhile, had been taken to Ealing police station. "From the beginning I didn't speak to them," she says. "I told them I wouldn't speak to them unless they recognized me as a fighter or POW. I don't know why I said that, but I didn't want to speak to anybody. I was in grief, first because Patrick was killed, and also because we failed with the hijacking, because that was the main one to release the prisoners." Khaled was also in pain; the ribs broken when she was jumped on in the airplane had been taped and she was bruised and battered.

Khaled maintained an abrasive attitude towards her captors for a good week. After five days of silent hostility, she finally began talking, to a police officer she names as Chief Superintendent David Frew. He had opened the conversation by granting her demand that she be recognized as a PFLP fighter. But when he started to ask more questions she responded by saying that, as she had been recognized as a fighter, all she had to do was give her name and unit, as is the case for formal prisoners of war. "We're not at war with you," said Frew. "You declared war on us in 1917, with the Balfour Declaration," was Khaled's riposte. The two played cat and mouse games, with Frew refusing to listen to Khaled's attempts to deliver political speeches, and Khaled insisting that the British authorities had no right to detain her.

But Frew had information which Khaled wanted. "It's not only you that hijacks planes, your comrades hijacked others," he told her. "I wanted to know about this," she confesses. "He began to say it quickly, Swissair, TWA, Pan Am, BOAC. I said, look, don't speak so fast, I may miss some of the English, and you may be mistaken mentioning four airplanes. So he named them again. And I said, BOAC was not in the plan." Frew told Khaled that the BOAC flight had been taken to Dawson's Field, but she didn't know what he meant. "I knew there was a big airfield," she says, "but I didn't know that name, we called it

Revolution Airport. So I asked, where is this Dawson's Field and why, what are their demands? He said: to release you.'

Frew didn't believe that the BOAC hijack could have been a spontaneous reaction to Khaled's imprisonment: he apparently thought that she must have known more than she was letting on, and that the news of her comrades' exploits might be enough to break her silence. He was largely correct. After some concessions from the British in recognizing her status as a fighter—and finding her some slippers for her cold feet—Khaled did indeed start to be more cooperative, and her daily life in Ealing police station improved. The whole building had been evacuated, she was told, apart from her, her interrogators and seven guards who accompanied her round-the-clock—including two in her cell at all times. But she was allowed exercise sessions and a female police officer was even allocated to play table tennis with her. She asked for reading material and, having angrily rejected the women's magazines she was first offered, was brought newspapers, with the apologetic explanation that they had been delayed by a strike.

According to Khaled, once she started communicating with the police, the atmosphere in the station was fairly relaxed. She describes a fair amount of joking around—asking her guards if they were in her cell all the time because they'd hijacked planes too, or naming the procession of guards who followed her every time she went upstairs to shower "The Queen's Parade." She was given the station chief's bathroom to wash in, and was brought clean clothes and towels, although she did renew her argumentative style when they tried to allocate a female guard to sit in the room with her as she showered. "I'm not going to kill myself," she told them. "I still have more missions to do."

When an even more senior police officer visited to view his unusual prisoner, she also joked that she had brought the sunny weather outside with her from the Middle East, and that she'd like to see some of it. He ordered his officers to take her to a higher floor and open up the windows to let her breathe the air.

Certainly Khaled seems to have retained a generally positive feeling towards Ealing police station and her time in it. She spent some of that time chatting with one of the women police officers about boyfriends, husbands, and divorces, and she appreciated the extra cigarettes friendly officers smuggled in to top up her ration of six a day. She later exchanged Christmas cards with some of the officers who had guarded her and corresponded with one for several years, until the Lebanese civil war disrupted the postal service. On a 2002 visit to the UK she visited the building and a friend took a photo of her in front of it; when a police officer from inside told them this wasn't allowed they simply told her that Khaled was a tourist. But the story made the *Guardian* newspaper a few days later.

According to Khaled, a fair amount of what appeared in the papers was coming from David Frew and his colleagues themselves. They taught her to play cards, but soon afterwards cartoons started to appear of her beating her guards and interrogators at poker and building a pile of her winnings from the British state. And after she told David Frew "look, I don't like men's compliments, you know that I'm an Arab woman and that we don't accept compliments from men," this also appeared in the press. "I saw this in the newspapers," says Khaled, "and I went to him and told him, you go and speak to the press but you don't give me the right to speak to them, why do you tell them to write these things? I think you are violating the rules. All the time I was telling him, you are violating the rules!" she laughs. "I think that he felt guilty. He was very nice in speaking to me, but it wasn't in our plan for me to be there, we didn't expect it this way."

Khaled also seems to have derived a certain satisfaction from quoting her legal rights at Frew and anyone else who tried to interrogate her. She cited the statutory rights of suspects at them—she had memorized these from the nineteenth-century regulations posted on the wall of her cell. And when three men from Scotland Yard tried to talk to her, she remained stubbornly silent until there was a woman officer present. The first policewoman who came was Hazel—"she's the only one whose name I remember now," says Khaled. This was an officer who had annoyed her on previous occasions, so she again sulked and refused to talk until a different female officer could be found.

It seems, though, that Khaled wasn't just trying to be awkward out of a sense of anti-authoritarian bloody-mindedness, but felt that she had to balance out the amiable relations she had with some of her captors by showing some defiance. "All the time, I was thinking about what to do and how to act," she says. "Comrades Ghassan Kanafani and Bassam Abu-Sharif from the PFLP were talking to the press in Jordan, saying that if Britain hurts a hair on her head you cannot know what we will do. So I had to think about how I would be." The British government, under pressure from all sides, seemed to have little, if any, intention of handing Khaled over to the Israelis. She even claims that "when I came back Ghassan Kanafani told me that the British ambassador came to the PFLP headquarters with the embassy emblem, off the front door, and the flag, and told him, 'take this as a hostage. Leila will be released.'"

Once she started receiving newspapers, Khaled, in her London cell, was reasonably aware of events in Jordan. She kept up a defiant front, telling David Frew about the clashes between the Palestinian guerrillas and the Hashemite regime earlier in 1970, in which she had taken part as a fighter. "We defended ourselves and after only a week it stopped," she boasted.

But as the conflict in Jordan continued, she grew more concerned. "I didn't want to show how disturbed I was," she says. "I wanted to keep myself solid, so I just kept reading. David Frew would come at night to discuss this with me—he said that if I wanted asylum I could ask for it, because the resistance was over. I told him that if it was over I will go home and have children and teach them to be fighters. I felt that they wanted to break my will, so I acted as if it was something I was used to, that I knew all about." "We were aware that this regime had a mission against us," Khaled continues. "They waited, but it was only a matter of time and they took the opportunity of the hijackings. But it was an excuse."

On September 28, however, the guards did see Khaled crying, when she heard of the death of Gamal Abdel Nasser. She heard the news as one of her guards listened to the radio just outside her cell. "They asked me, why are you crying," says Khaled. "David Frew came that night and he asked, you didn't cry when your people were killed, why are you crying now?" She explained to him that Nasser was a national leader to her. The guerrillas expected to be killed, but Nasser was a political leader who, she felt, had achieved a lot for Arab unity and for the Palestinians. "But I also cried when Kennedy was assassinated," she says, also recognizing him as an important political leader of his nation. "Frew said, really? You cried? I said yes, because I'm against assassination, and the next day I saw it in the newspapers, they put it in the newspapers that I said I cried because of Kennedy."

The reaction of the British press to the Palestinian hijacker imprisoned in one of their police stations was surprisingly benign. Headlines usually referred to Khaled as "Leila" or "Hijack Girl," or in some of the more sober publications, "Miss Khaled." She herself was rarely criticized for her part in the hijackings, although the commandos on the ground were portrayed as more sinister figures. Most discussions of Khaled herself mentioned her health and weighed up the likelihood of her imminent release. The main topic of interest for personalized reporting of the saga tended to be the Western hostages in Amman and the conflict conditions under which the respectable "sons and daughters of diplomats ... being escorted by Mrs Lesley Cooke of Pimlico" were being kept.[43] The British public were also apparently interested in Leila; she received bundles of letters, including both hate mail and marriage proposals. She wasn't allowed to reply to British correspondents, but she was permitted to write to her family.[44]

Finally, on September 30, after weeks of negotiations between the British government and the PFLP, the Jordanian authorities and the other countries with civilians on the hijacked planes, Khaled was released. Flippant to the end, she told David Frew, "I like this hotel, it is awarded ten stars; the service is very good and I will ask my comrades to come here." That Christmas, she sent him and some of the other police guards cards featuring mock plane tickets and photographs of the exploded aircraft at Dawson's Field. Even getting her out of Ealing was complex; she was told to walk straight out of the door and lie down in the back of the waiting Land Rover (or by some accounts a black police van). Dressed in dark uniform like a policewoman, she managed to evade the waiting press corps.[45]

With the police vehicle accompanied by motorcycle outriders and squad cars, Khaled was transported to Northolt aerodrome to be taken by helicopter to RAF Lyneham.[46] There she was put on an RAF Comet, which also collected Palestinian prisoners from Munich and Zurich who had been bargained for German and Swiss hostages. Arriving in Cairo on the morning of October 1, Khaled, the released Palestinian prisoners, and some of the commandos from Dawson's Field were held in a safe house for 11 days.[47] Khaled, though, was itching to return to front-line operations, not realizing that this time her even greater notoriety really would confine her. But before they left, the group went to lay a wreath on the grave of Gamal Abdel Nasser. Khaled, wearing a black trouser suit and dark glasses, was asked by ITN's Michael Brunson if she felt responsible for igniting the conflagration which had consumed so much of the Middle East in the previous weeks. "Not at all," she said.[48]

"I went from Cairo to Syria with the other comrades," says Khaled simply, "with the other comrades who were in European jails. Then we went to Lebanon because the PLO fighters had been driven out of Jordan to Lebanon."

4

Marriage and Death

In Lebanon, Khaled returned to her "assigned mission" with Wadi'a Haddad's external operations unit of the PFLP. But, she recalls, "The whole situation was in a mess because after the fighters and the PLO went to Beirut it took time to rearrange everything there, to build the bases in the south." And although it's often assumed that there was a clean break with Jordan, the resistance organizations spent many months trying to maintain some positions there, whilst building up their new presence in Lebanon. As Rayyes and Nahas described the situation five years later:

> By the spring of 1971, the commandos were effectively limited to their last strongholds in the Jerash and Ajloun areas of northern Jordan. The thoroughness with which the Jordanian Army proceeded to eliminate them in July 1971 caught the Palestinian leadership off balance and removed the guerrillas as an effective force in Jordan for the immediate future. By the end of 1971 the resistance was dead in Jordan and in a critical condition in the rest of the Middle East.[1]

The PFLP's rigorous line on work meant that Khaled wasn't granted any time off on her return from captivity in London. She recalls that "My mother came from the south where she was living, in Tyre, and she wanted to see me. So I went to my sister's house. And Dr Wadi'a told me 'you have 15 minutes to see your mother.' I said 'how come? I have to stay with her overnight.' So he came with me, because he was very well known to my family, because at the time of the Arab Nationalist Movement the leadership used to come and have meetings in our house in the south in the 1950s and '60s. My mother told him, 'let her stay with us tonight.' But he said 'no, because she had a long vacation' and I said 'vacation, in prison!' He replied to me, 'what were you doing there? Nothing. So you have to go back to work directly.' So we stayed more than 15 minutes of course, but I had to go."

But, says Khaled, Wadi'a Haddad's hard-line stance didn't just stem from the desire to get her back to work. "It was dangerous to stay in one place," she says, "so I was always moving from one place to another because every now and then the Israelis would say 'we're not going to let her find a safe place in Beirut.' They kept sending these statements, so I had to move, and this of course meant that I'm not stable in one place, but at the same time I had to go to the meetings in different places to build the movement."

During the 1960s, Beirut, where the main PLO organizations formed their new bases, had been a cosmopolitan holiday destination. As the eminent war journalist Robert Fisk described it:

> The economy continued to grow, the banking services increased; by 1962, 38 airlines were flying into Beirut at the rate of 99 flights a day. It was calculated that 65,000 of the country's registered 76,000 road vehicles were used by or for tourists. "Beirut ... is acquitting herself brilliantly in her new role of tourist "Gateway to the East," Hachette's Guide to Lebanon boldly announced in 1965.[2]

But power and wealth in the outwardly successful "rainbow" Lebanon, with its mixed communities, were immensely unequally distributed along ethnic, sectarian and gender lines,[3] and the addition of thousands of Palestinian fighters to the mix increased the tensions which lurked under the surface.

This was an internationally accessible yet volatile environment, close to the conflict zone on the Israeli-Lebanese border and to the training camps in the mountains frequented by both the Palestinian factions and their international supporters. Leila Khaled and her comrades helped to create a radical scene, aided by the fact that Lebanon had one of the most open media in the region and at the time provided a refuge for figures from opposition movements across the Arab world and beyond. As well as the recruiting grounds represented by the large Palestinian refugee camps, Beirut was also home to a plethora of other groups. In his biography of his Armenian nationalist brother Monte, Markar Melkonian describes a violent, exciting world of 1970s Beirut, peppered with personalities—including Leila Khaled and Wadi'a Haddad—and where armed revolutionary groups from all around the world shared knowledge, experience, and personnel.[4] "Many foreigners came to work with us, from different countries, some of them from organizations" says Khaled. "Patrick [Arguello] was from the Sandinistas, we had relations with them. The Palestinian cause attracted many of the oppositional groups and liberation movements, to the different factions of the Palestinian Resistance—Fatah, the PFLP. Before I knew it, people were beginning to come to meet us, to be trained, from Europe, America, Japan." Some were there to fight for Palestine; others were being trained by the rebels in a spirit of leftist internationalism, and would take the skills they learned to other struggles.

Some of these international contacts cast doubt on the commitment to avoiding violence against civilians and concentrating on Israeli military targets which Leila Khaled and current PFLP spokesman Khalil Meqdisi stress in interviews and statements. In 1972, for instance, Japanese Red Army gunmen shot dead 24 people, mainly civilians, at Lod airport. The men had trained with the PFLP and travelled to the Middle East via Lebanon and one of those who died in the raid was married to Red Army member Fusako Shigenobe, who had been photographed with Leila Khaled in Beirut a few days before the killings. One of the guerrillas, Kozo Okamoto, failed to go through with the suicide pact the group had apparently made before the operation and was captured by Israeli security forces, before being subjected to long periods of torture and imprisonment in isolation. He named "Basam Towfik Sheriff" (a confused version of the name of Bassam Tawfiq Abu-Sharif, the PFLP's spokesman at Dawson's Field) as one of his contacts while he was staying in a safe house in Beirut.[5]

In 1970, the PFLP's Central Committee decided to halt airplane hijackings, but Wadi'a Haddad disagreed with this move. In

1976, he organized the Entebbe operation, for which, according to Khaled, he was expelled from the PFLP (some versions say that he left before this, possibly as early as 1972[6]). At Entebbe, Israeli commandos, including Benjamin Netanyahu's brother Yonatan, killed the hijackers and some of the hostages. Some of the Israelis were also killed, including Yonatan Netanyahu. Haddad maintained relations with some PFLP members until his death from cancer in a German hospital in 1978. The PFLP paid tribute to him and a delegation led by George Habash attended his funeral in Iraq, where he was buried.[7] The Rejection Front, the coalition of Palestinian factions which opposed Arafat's leanings towards dialogue with Israel, includes both the PFLP and more specifically violent organizations. These include the PFLP-General Command, the organization led by Ahmed Jibril which eschewed hijackings and hostage releases in favor of mid-air bombings with hundreds of casualties, and which is regularly named in conspiracy theories about the Lockerbie-Pan Am airplane bombing.[8]

One of the Beirut personalities of the radical years of the 1970s was, of course, Yasser Arafat, of the PFLP's main rival and PLO partner, Fatah. Over the years, Khaled was to come to know him well through her role on the Palestine National Council and in the General Union of Palestinian Women (al-Ittihad al-'Am lil-Mara al-Filastini). "We established a house in Tel el-Za'atar camp for the children," she says, "and often he came to have dinner or lunch there and find out about the children. Sometimes we discussed different political attitudes, sometimes he tried to tell us that the PLO leadership decided the political positions. I told him, this is dictatorship, don't you think so? Aren't we a democratic people? He always said that Palestinian democracy is a world of guns, it must be a balance between democracy and arms. He was a very pragmatic person, very charismatic, active and dynamic, but at the same time he does what he thinks is right, even if others on the committees or from different groups have discussed and discussed, he would still take the decision by himself. Once he declared it. He said, you speak what you want and I'll do what I want."

Sometimes working with Arafat and sometimes at conflict with him was another of the PLO heavyweights, PFLP General Secretary George Habash. Khaled worked with him for over 40 years until his death in January 2008, and she still speaks of him with great respect and quiet emotion. Known to many in the resistance as Al-Hakim, "the doctor," a reference both to his medical training and his reputation for wisdom, Khaled contrasts his leadership style with that of Arafat. "He discusses and then takes the position of the majority," she claims. "He was a wise kind of man, very enthusiastic and also charismatic in his way. He would listen very closely when you talked to him, and then give an answer. I never saw him shouting or screaming. He once said to me 'when you get angry you have to use your anger against the main [problem], which is the enemy, so you shouldn't be angry or nervous as long as Palestine is occupied.'"

"He was always very passionate," she continues. "Many times I saw him crying, just silently, when we spoke about the children or the mothers of martyrs, or even in his later years if someone sent their greetings from the Occupied Territories. And he was a very solid person, and I learnt a lot from him. He was the kind of man who, even if you are in contradiction with his ideas you can't feel anything but love and respect for him. Even Arafat always said, we disagree but he is a brother in the struggle. I think even at that time he was the conscience of the revolution." Even whilst discussing Habash in the context of the PFLP as "an extreme example of a personality cult," As'ad AbuKhalil concedes that he was a man of "enormous charisma and popularity" despite the sometimes "authoritarian" nature of his leadership and the "shattering" effect of his rivalry with DFLP founder Nayef Hawatmeh.[9]

*   *   *

Despite her commitment, Khaled acknowledges that the dangerous, unsettled life she was leading took a toll on her personally. Before her 1970 mission, Bassim, the commander of the military camp where she had been based, proposed to her. They had, she recorded in her 1973 autobiography, started falling in love while she was at her first PFLP training camp in Jordan in the summer of 1969. The matter-of-fact language and political statements of *My People Shall Live* suddenly shifts into romantic mode as she writes that "I, along with our squad commander, Bassim, were frequent visitors [to a Bedouin community near the training camp in the Jordanian hills] and occasionally we were invited as guests to their feasts. I remember vividly the night we attended a wedding dinner celebrated before the parents of the bride took their daughter to the groom's tent. A desert moon whispered love to those assembled; it was a night to love and be loved. Gracious maidens danced, their flowing rainbow, coloured robes touching our cheeks gently. All was joy, all was fun. Bassim and I were beginning to fall in love." By February 1970 they were engaged—at the approval of the PFLP, although neither family had been consulted—and that spring Bassim's sister Samirah was sent to Jordan to take a look at her. Khaled had to juggle her role as a fighter with shepherding her (fortunately hardy) future sister-in-law around an Amman littered with burning vehicles and bursts of gunfire, as the fedayeen clashed with Hashemite forces.[10]

Bassim was an Iraqi who had joined the PFLP in 1968 after being jailed for ten years for Communist Party membership in Iraq: "I said yes," says Khaled of his proposal. "Everybody was asking, how are you going to live together? and I said 'it's not a problem, he goes to his work and I go to my work and that's it.' Even my family were asking, what kind of marriage is this? How is it going to be? And I said, it's OK. I thought that as long as we are struggling for a cause then this is the base on which we can build a relationship and a marriage."

There was little romance to Khaled's wedding. Her husband had to request permission from the PFLP's leadership and there was, she recalls, "no party." Her autobiography gives the date as November 26, but reports in the Western press pre-date this by several weeks, suggesting that her life story is in error. But 35 years later her face and manner still showed some of the excitement of a young woman who, despite—or perhaps because of—her guerilla training, thought that she had found a new way to be in love. "He was the first one to train me to hold arms," she recalls, "so I looked on him as a god. It was for me something I hadn't dared dream of, just to bear arms. So he had trained me in this, and when he proposed to me I said yes directly, with no hesitation."

Despite the low-key ceremony, the event—just a month after her return from British custody—warranted coverage in the international press. "Leila Khaled, age 25, who unsuccessfully tried to hijack an El Al airliner, has married a fellow guerrilla, code name Baasem, an Iraqui [sic], who was once her instructor in unarmed combat," reported the *Guardian* newspaper on November 7, 1970. "Married. Leila Khaled, 24, nervy Palestinian commando and a central figure in the multiplane hijacking last September; and a guerrilla identified only as Bassem; in Amman, Jordan," noted *Time* magazine on November 16.

The couple were permitted a week's honeymoon to visit his family in Iraq. Then her new husband returned to his role in a PFLP base in Jordan, and Khaled went back to Lebanon. They saw each other again for three days, three months later. And again, after another three months, he came to visit in July 1971. "We had to arrange all this through our leadership," Khaled recalls, "so that I could arrange to be in Beirut and not somewhere else."

But, just as Bassim arrived in Beirut, fighting between Palestinian fedayeen and the Hashemite regime broke out again in Jordan and he was, says Khaled, "furious" not to be on the ground with his men. He told her: "'It's because of you that I'm not there, I have to go back.' So I said, OK, you can go back. He was responsible for many of the fighters and the news came out that they are killed, so it was difficult for him and for me of course, but more for him because he was the one who was responsible for them. So he went to Syria and over the border to northern Jordan."

This incident didn't immediately spell the end of the marriage, but it heralded its decline. Khaled, she says, "realized that we cannot cope, because we don't sit together, we don't live together, and I began to realize that there are many contradictions between my ideas and his ideas, the way we live." Khaled herself had to move around and sometimes leave Lebanon on PFLP missions, and in 1972 Bassim was sent to China for six months on what Khaled described as a "training course"—at this time China was regularly supplying the Palestinian resistance with arms and military training.[11] As a result, the couple didn't see each other for over a year. Eventually they met, but "like two people without any relationship between them."

Just a week after their ambivalent reunion, Israeli threats intervened in Khaled's personal life again. On July 8, 1972, Ghassan Kanafani, a renowned Palestinian writer, editor of several of the PFLP's publications over the years and a major figure in the Party, was assassinated (along with his teenage niece) by a Mossad car bomb. The killing was just one of a spate of Israeli assassination attempts against senior PFLP and other PLO figures, which also included a letter-bomb attack on party spokesman Bassam Abu-Sharif—who had been prominent at Dawson's Field—which disfigured and nearly blinded him and removed several fingers.[12] The PFLP, probably rightly, read Kanafani's assassination as a threat to other high-profile members of the party and ordered Leila Khaled underground.

"Our leadership said that I had to hide," Khaled recalls, "and they instituted security measures for me. And Bassim said to me 'I'm not going to be with you,' so that was the end of it. I said to him that these measures are for me, not for you, but he said he wasn't going to accept it, so that was it. We had to get divorced. He didn't accept the divorce, but we managed. For me, I had to stop and think that if my partner is not going to take responsibility with me according to the dangers and the challenges we are facing, then what kind of relationship are we having? So, we spoke to our party leadership and told them that we had to have a divorce, and we parted, and we didn't see each other again." Khaled remains calm and dignified as she speaks of the failure of her first marriage, although a little regret seeps out; even her most personal affairs must fit, it seems, within the framework of her revolutionary commitments.

"It's difficult being divorced in our society," Khaled concedes. "Especially when there are children, but still. So, it depends firstly on the woman, how she faces it, but also her family, how she faces them, not to leave them without speaking a word, as if it's something she's ashamed of. At the same time, we have to have respect for the society that we are living in." After decades of seeing marriages amongst her militant comrades fail, Khaled emphasizes that for a politically active woman, "if she's married, she had to be very clear to her partner when she has to go and do something. My first marriage failed because we didn't think of speaking about different issues. We thought that we were freedom fighters so it would be OK, but this is not the basis for a life."

Despite the Israeli threat to Leila Khaled, the PFLP had apparently decided that it wanted to grasp the opportunity presented by her fame—or notoriety—which had been increased beyond measure by her sojourn in a London police station. A Lebanese academic, George Hajjar, who was at the time teaching in a Canadian university, proposed in 1970 that he ghost-write Khaled's autobiography with her. From the PFLP's perspective, a book written from the Palestinian perspective was politically desirable, and with their star hijacker as a selling point it could be invaluable in getting their message across.

Hajjar came to Lebanon and recorded Leila Khaled's account of her life story, and as Hajjar wrote she then reviewed each chapter with Ghassan Kanafani. As they were finishing the manuscript they heard from Hajjar, back in Canada. A Zionist organization in the USA had taken legal action against the American publishers with whom he had a contract, and were also planning to sue him personally. According to Khaled, in the USA they successfully argued that the book promoted terrorism and they lost their contract there in 1972. Hajjar and the PFLP were also forced to pay court costs. In the controversy, Hajjar was also fired from his university in Canada and, Khaled alleges, on his return to Beirut was also denied a post at the American University because of the book. In 1973 Hodder & Stoughton picked up the manuscript and *My People Shall Live* was published in the UK, to mixed reviews and success. When leading book chain W. H. Smith stated that it wasn't going to stock the book it made minor headlines, but the company insisted that it just "didn't think it was going to sell well."[13] It has, however, been widely translated for pirate editions in

French, in Arabic by a Lebanese publisher, and in Urdu and Japanese. Original copies now exchange hands for hundreds of pounds, and PDFs of the full book are now widely available on the internet.

*   *   *

As well as the threat to Leila Khaled and her comrades from Israeli operations, the Palestinian population of Lebanon was in growing danger from the increasing tensions across the country. The Palestinians were just one problem amongst many in a country cross-cut by faith as well as class and political allegiances and outside interventions, from neighbors such as Syria as well as Western states. In 1973, Khaled recounts, "the Lebanese army besieged the camps in Beirut. I was in a place in the Eastern part of Beirut, where it was very dangerous for me to be seen, so I had to cross the city that day and return to the camps."

In coming years, the journey from West to East Beirut was to become one of the most notoriously dangerous in the world. On this day in 1973, Leila Khaled had to use her ingenuity and guts and some sheer bullying to get herself and the PFLP munitions she was looking after across the city: "The woman whose house I was in, she was pregnant. Her husband was at work in a restaurant, the army was everywhere, and there was no one there but her and me. So I told her, look, now I'm your maid, I'll put on a headscarf and you pretend that you are going to deliver the baby. I went to the balcony and started to scream, and the soldiers asked what was wrong. I cried 'please bring us an ambulance, this woman is going to deliver.' I did all this because there were weapons in the house. She didn't know about them, but her husband did. I put the weapons on a sheet, put her on top of them, and told her "don't say anything, just scream!" And she was screaming not because of the baby but because she was afraid. Two men came and put her in the car, still screaming, and I was screaming too, and they took us to West Beirut. We went to the restaurant and I said to the husband, take your wife! And I took the weapons."

Khaled spent the month or so of clashes in 1973 living in the refugee camps of Bourj al-Barajneh and Shatila, later to become notorious for massacres carried out by the Israeli-backed Maronite Christian Phalangists in 1982. Khaled herself was relying on the camps, dangerous as they were, because they seemed the least likely place anyone would try to find her. On this occasion, the fighting was ended with a controversial agreement that the Lebanese army would not besiege the camps or prevent Palestinian fighters from operating in them.

Leila Khaled in a refugee camp in Beirut, circa 1974–5
(Terry Fincher / Getty Images).

Leila Khaled was now leading a very different life from that of the high-profile hijacker and star of Wadi'a Haddad's external operations unit. In 1970 a meeting of the PFLP's Central Committee had called an end to airplane hijacking as a tactic, declaring that the technique had accomplished its aim of bringing the plight of the Palestinians to the world's notice. According to Khaled, they also felt that to carry on hijacking planes would now be counter-productive and too controversial. So Khaled's unique expertise no longer had the same relevance.

"At the same time," says Khaled, "this section of the PFLP moved, and I said I don't want to go too, I'll stay in Beirut. Also, I felt that I was being focused on too much. It felt like everybody looked on me as if I was somehow different from my comrades. This made me think that I shouldn't be in the spotlight any more, that I didn't want to feel that I was somehow in a different category from them and get too proud." Khaled's solution was to request that she be allowed to go and live in the refugee camps in Beirut. "I wanted to go to have a new mission," she explains. "We needed to organize, to lead ourselves, for a new generation."

*   *   *

Also in 1973, Khaled began her involvement in the Palestinian women's movement, a career which has—as we will see later—been controversial, but which occupied much of her life in the late 1970s and 1980s.

By 1975, a full-blown civil war had developed in Lebanon, with the Palestinians just one involved in the many shifting alliances of heavily armed forces. "There were many strikes," recalls Khaled. "The workers, farmers, students. And one of the prominent parliamentarians in the South, Maarouf Saad, went on a demonstration with the fishermen in the south, in Saida where he was Mayor. They had their own demands of the government, but he was shot dead. That was in 1975." Another key moment in the increasing tension was the attack by Phalangist forces on a busload of Palestinians returning to West Beirut from a political rally in Tel al-Za'atar camp.

Leila Khaled was acting as one of the PFLP's representatives in the General Union of Palestinian Women, but was also part of the armed resistance which tried to protect the refugee camps from the Lebanese army and right-wing Christian militia incursions.

On Christmas day 1976, however, Khaled's notoriety had its greatest impact yet on her family. Returning to her apartment one morning, she found her sister and her sister's fiancé shot dead. The gunmen's intended target was Khaled herself.

In 2008, a visibly distressed Khaled described the incident: "At the end of 1976 my sister and her fiancé were assassinated in my house. I was out. It was the 25th of December. It had been declared that the war had stopped, and the Syrians came in with their troops. We had been instructed not to sleep in our houses because it could be dangerous, because it was Christmas night and maybe the Phalangists were planning something. So I told my sister not to stay, because she was living with me in the apartment. We didn't really live there, we just put our things there and then went out because we were so busy. Sometimes we would sleep there."

"My sister and her fiancé had arranged to get married. But according to my mother, we weren't allowed to have a wedding party. She had told us a long time before, big wedding parties and the woman wearing a white dress—this could only happen in Haifa [because no personal event could be properly celebrated until the family, as refugees, could return home]. And of course it was the war so this was another reason we shouldn't have a party. But to have a substitute, she was going to hold a dinner at our house in Tyre, for the wedding party and for the comrades, especially those whose mothers were in the Occupied Territories. So, that incident was shocking and sickening for me. I arranged with my sister to meet at 10 o'clock in the morning to go to Tyre for the wedding party. In Lebanon at that time, especially in Beirut, if you give a time you have to be exactly right, if you are a minute or five minutes late it means that you've been kidnapped, because this is the way things happen, so one should be very exact. So I came, and the apartment was on the eighth floor. I saw my sister's car, so I thought, it's 10 o'clock, she is there."

"There was no lift, no electricity, so I climbed. I saw that the door was open, and I said 'aren't you ashamed to keep the door open?,' because we had four locks, everywhere security is like this. I went into the sitting room. My sister's fiancé was sitting with his arms open. She was lying down. In that house, there was a dark colored rug, so I didn't see her blood. He was shot in the head, his forehead was open, but I didn't see the blood, I saw him sitting. So I came and sat beside him. I looked at him and asked, why are you silent? I was speaking to my sister: did you tumble down? Were you sitting on his lap? I thought this way. My mind did not accept what I saw.

Then I said, 'let's go!' and because of course he didn't answer me, I was looking at him, asking, 'why don't you answer me? We arranged to go today to Tyre, so let's go now.' But then I saw some drops of the blood on the wall. All the blood on the floor I didn't see, but I saw this. I began to scream, I put my hand on my sister, but I didn't see any blood on her, she was shot and she was on the floor. So I got my pistol and ran down, thinking that I knew who had killed them, and I wanted to go and kill them. But after about two storeys, I came back."

Apparently confused and almost hallucinating in her distress, Khaled says "I was worried that they [her sister and her fiancé] will be killed another time. A woman from the building said 'what's wrong?' and I told her. And then I had to go to my other sister's house and tell her, and she was shocked because she thought that I was killed. And all the time, I had told my mother to be prepared for my death, that this is the way I chose to live so she shouldn't react negatively. I thought it would be me and not my sister. She said 'what do you mean?' And I said you should say she is a martyr, and be proud of her. Now, I know that this was very difficult for a mother. And this was very difficult for me."

Discussions with her comrades in the PFLP convinced Khaled that the killings had been carried out by double agents, Phalangists or Israeli operatives working within the PFLP. As a result, she refused to carry on working for the party until the killers were caught and the truth made public—a process which took a year.

Devastated by her loss and needing to escape the continuous pressure of war-torn Lebanon, Khaled went to stay with her brothers in the Gulf. But even then she couldn't sleep or eat, so she returned to Lebanon and went to stay with her mother in Tyre. The PFLP leadership assured her that they were investigating the assassinations and even her mother, Khaled says, told her that "you have to go and join your work, this is your belief." But, she says, "I couldn't do it, I couldn't do anything."

In 1978 Israel invaded Lebanon and Khaled finally returned to Beirut from Tyre. She worked with the GUPW and other women's organizations to help house the thousands of displaced people flooding north from the area under Israeli attack. "It was really a big mess in the area and day and night we had to go from one place to another to work," Khaled recalls. She also admits that although she wanted to play a role in the armed struggle at the time, she was not permitted to, perhaps because the PFLP leadership recognized her fragile state. So, she says, "My mission was with the union, because I was one of the members of the leadership of the Union."

Leila Khaled's escape from the horrors of Lebanon and the grief of her family life came through her work with international socialist women's organizations. At a conference of the Democratic Women's Federation in Moscow in the summer of 1978, in a Palestinian delegation meeting with the Soviet committee, Valentina Tereshkova asked Khaled where she had studied. Her family's lack of money meant that Khaled never completed the pharmacy course she had started at the American University of Beirut in the mid 1960s, so Tereshkova suggested that on her return to Beirut, Khaled send in her papers to apply for a place at a Soviet university.

"They thought that I was very young, that it was only two years that I finished school," recalls Khaled. "I looked very young at that time. But it was sixteen years since I left school. So I sent them my papers, and of course the Ministry didn't accept me, because it was a long time since I had been at school. But the women's committee had promised me, so they had to let me come."

During the 1970s, the Soviet bloc gave large numbers of scholarships to students from around the world, training doctors, engineers, and pharmacists from socialist and non-aligned countries across Latin America, Africa, and Asia. If she had asked to study one of these subjects, with places in high demand, Leila Khaled's story might have been different. But she applied to study history. And, she says, "nobody goes to study history in another country, so they accepted me."

Like many people who have been denied an education when they wanted one, and like many Palestinians, from one of the best-educated populations in the Middle East, Leila Khaled threw herself into her studies. For her first year in the Soviet Union, 1978–79, she was required to learn Russian to a high enough level to study in the language for a further three years. "Sometimes I was the only one to go to class," she recalls. "The others didn't come and the teacher had to wait for them, so we would discuss other things." According to Khaled, Tereshkova's committee which had recommended her for the place kept a close eye on her, contacting the university authorities, only to be told "she's the only one who's really committed to her classes." "It's difficult after sixteen years to start going to classes again," says Khaled, "and I acted like a kindergarten child, studying and writing my homework. It was a good experience for me."

Also at university in the USSR in 1978 was fellow PFLP member Fayez Hilal, a medical student. Although he was in his final year he and Khaled got to know each other, as PFLP members studying in the same country were expected to help and support one another, and Fayez was assigned to her. Despite a caution inspired by her unfortunate first marriage, Leila Khaled and Fayez Hilal found feelings which she seems not to have expected to experience again growing between them.

"In 1979, Fayez was also attending a conference of the General Union of Palestinian Students in Lebanon," Khaled recalls. "Then he came back to the Soviet Union, and we began to deal with each other as, well, as comrades, but also there was a kind of passion. We didn't decide anything, but this relationship developed."

Fayez graduated in 1979, and when Khaled came back to Lebanon at the end of the university year he suggested that they speak to the party leadership because, as Khaled puts it "we discuss everything in the party, even on a private level."

Discouraged by her earlier experiences, Khaled stalled, saying that it was still early in their relationship and that she still had several years of study in the USSR to complete. "I thought, let's test this relationship before we decide, let's test it when we're apart. And because I had my experience of my first marriage, I was afraid another marriage will fail too, so I was very cautious."

So Fayez Hilal returned to Jordan, telling the Jordanian authorities that he had lost his passport in the USSR so that he could enter the country and open the medical clinic he'd been planning there. Leila Khaled, meanwhile, returned to the Soviet Union, where her notoriety had again caught up with her. Nineteen-eighty was the year of the Moscow Olympics; the USSR was on the receiving end of a major political and media attack, led by the Reagan administration's boycott calls, and having a former airplane hijacker wandering the streets of their capital was not to the Russians' taste.

Khaled protested that she was also in Moscow as a representative of the General Union of Palestinian Women, and that Soviet travel restrictions—which meant that foreign students were issued with documents for the city they were assigned to and could not move around the country—would prevent her doing her job. The Soviet authorities wanted to send her to Rostov, 200 kilometers away, and insisted that the university there specialized in the humanities subjects that she was studying. At a conference on the subject of children, at which Khaled was leading the Palestinian delegation, Vilma Espin, president of the Cuban Women's Committee and the wife of Raul Castro, stirred the controversy further by suggesting to Khaled that she should continue her studies in Cuba instead.

Finally the General Union of Palestinian Women told Khaled not to make a fuss and to accept a year's transfer to Rostov. One of Khaled's new friends in Moscow, a Russian language teacher whose husband was a senior party official at Moscow University, finally told her the Soviet government's reasons for wanting her out of Moscow for the year. "If you want to help, you'll go to Rostov," she was told. Complying with party discipline as she had on other occasions, she obeyed. But, she says, "The students, they were very young, 19 or 20, just finishing school and coming to university. It was difficult for me, working with students this age. I was 35 years old."

But, as with her early studies in Beirut, Leila Khaled never reached the end of her degree. In 1980 Israeli military incursions into Lebanon increased and all PLO commandos were recalled, whatever they were doing and wherever they were. At the beginning of the year she had already clashed with the PFLP leadership over whether she should return to her studies or remain in Lebanon to prepare for the PFLP's conference, a major event in the party. She'd won that argument, but with Israeli raids escalating and her fellow students also heading back to the Middle East, she was compelled to join them. Although the PLO students were given official leave from their Soviet universities and would be allowed back to complete their studies, Khaled never returned.

In 1981 the confrontation with Israel escalated further. The bridges connecting Beirut and the South of Lebanon were bombed, and the situation for the Palestinian resistance was increasingly dangerous. In the midst of this, Fayez arrived. He and Leila had been writing to one another occasionally, although with both of them moving from country to country this was difficult. But he had heard that Khaled had received threats in Copenhagen and about the situation in Lebanon, and he was worried. To her surprise, he proposed. Cautious as ever, she told him to wait, pointing out that she was supposed to be continuing her degree in the USSR. He intended to find somewhere to specialize in his medical studies, so she suggested that he apply to return to Russia and they could meet again there. And, of course, they had to apply for permission from the PFLP leadership.

The following year, with the war between the Israelis, Palestinians, and various Lebanese forces in one of its bloodiest phases, Leila and Fayez had barely been able to keep in touch, so when he appeared again in March 1982 she wasn't expecting him. Reaching her in Beirut had been a struggle; Jordanian intelligence had confiscated his passport on the way. And then Fayez had had to face his prospective mother-in-law's advice, too.

"I was working in one of our offices, and one day I came home for lunch and found Fayez there. It was a big surprise to find him in my house," describes Leila Khaled. "My mother was telling him, why do you want to marry her? She is always busy. If my son wanted to marry a woman like this I wouldn't accept it. So because your mother is not here, I am your mother, and I'm advising you not to marry her." Fayez had been a PFLP activist in the West Bank and had been jailed and then deported by the Israeli authorities in 1970; he had been unable to see his family since.

"I said, why?" Khaled continues. "I'm not a bad person. I think I'm a good person? My mother said, 'I know, but you can't live like other women.' Fayez told her that he was also a member of the PFLP, that he had been jailed by the Israelis and so on, but she said, 'yes, I know, but she has already had an experience like this, he was the chief of a training camp and look what happened!' You see, in our society, women are afraid of being divorced and if she is, she is always followed to see how she is behaving. If a marriage fails, they blame the woman. I didn't care about being divorced, I was struggling, fighting, working, so it didn't cause me any problems, but it did cause them for my family. But I didn't know that because I wasn't living with them."

Despite her mother's efforts on his behalf, Leila Khaled and Fayez Hilal did arrange to marry. Typically, it wasn't a simple operation, starting with their visit to the sheikh to agree the legal aspects of the marriage. She had a Lebanese passport, but Fayez had had his confiscated by the Jordanians. He was given papers by the PLO, but the sheikh looked at them and said "what is this? This is not a proper identity paper." Fayez tried to explain that he was from the Occupied Territories and had no passport, that these were all the papers he had. But only when Khaled threatened to find someone else to carry out the wedding did the sheikh—who was friends with her family—agree to marry them.

Having overcome the hurdle of papers and identities (all-too-common for many Palestinians, not just fighters), the couple and the sheikh now clashed over their respective values: "so, the sheikh says OK, he goes to open the book, he writes down the names, and then he said, 'how much money?'" recounts Khaled. "Because in Islam, the woman is given money by the man, so that she has something left if she is divorced. He said, 'how much money do you want?' I told him, 'I don't want money. I'm not a product. You know me—I lead fighters, I'm responsible for people who go and die in the struggle. I don't want money.' He said, 'no, no, no,' and he closed the book. He told me, 'if you want to get married, you have to accept this.' Fayez came to ask what we were discussing and I said, 'I can't accept this.' So he said, 'OK, one lira.' I said to Fayez, 'give me the lira!' And he handed it over. The sheikh said, 'what do you want to be given afterwards?' And I said, one lira. He looked at me and said, 'you are weird.' I said, 'so I am weird! Write it down!'"

With the legal preamble sorted out, the wedding itself was similarly chaotic. Khaled's brother-in-law was assigned to bring the sheikh from Tyre, along with Khaled's papers, and they were scheduled to arrive at around 11 a.m. or noon. At half past eight in the morning there was a knock on Khaled's door; it was her brother-in-law with the sheikh, who had been in the bomb shelter all night and hadn't slept. The Tyre contingent of the family had taken advantage of a lull in the fierce Israeli shelling of their city, situated in the South of Lebanon, and travelled when it was safe—but not when it was planned. "So, I phoned the office and told them, 'go and find the bridegroom!' It was funny," says Khaled of a wedding day that would have made many brides faint with horror. "And in Islam you have to have two witnesses, so I said to some of the people in the office, 'come, we need witnesses.' They asked, 'where is Fayez? Has he been arrested?' And I said, 'you could say that he's being arrested—he's getting married.'"

Although she jokes about it now, Khaled has a serious point. "We don't live the same life as other people," she says of herself, Fayez, and their PFLP comrades. Like her assassinated sister— and even more so because of her death—Leila Khaled was forbidden by her mother to have a "white wedding" or a party. And Fayez also wanted to let his own family, un-contactable in the West Bank, know that he was married. This meant leaving Lebanon, which had no telephone connections with its enemy, Israel, so the couple managed to get permission to take a week's honeymoon in Bulgaria.

By this time, Fayez's mother was paralyzed, and she hadn't seen him in the 12 years since he was deported, although they had managed to speak on the telephone when he was studying in the USSR. "When he called her he was crying, she was crying, and I was crying because we got married and she couldn't see her son," says Khaled. "Because she was paralyzed she couldn't speak, and Fayez couldn't speak because he was crying. So I took the phone to say hello and she managed to say two words—'Biddi Bader'—I want Bader—she wanted us to have a child and name him Bader."

That was in May 1982. During their attempt at a honeymoon, Khaled fell ill and had to be taken to hospital, and they were beset with rumors about a planned all-out Israeli invasion of Lebanon. Khaled insisted that they return—and just a few days later the invasion took place. "It was," she says, "very terrible."

By the end of the month Khaled also knew that she was pregnant—which is why she had been ill and bleeding in Bulgaria, although the doctors there had not spotted it. Medics in Beirut told her that she had to lie down for three months, a notion which still causes her to laugh bitterly. Her mother had also been taken ill, with attacks of the stress-induced asthma which she had suffered from ever since the murder of Leila's sister in 1976. And Fayez, along with all other doctors, had been ordered to report directly to the nearest hospital. The couple arrived in Beirut on June 4, the day that the war began in earnest.

Concerned for both his pregnant wife and her mother, Fayez suggested that they join Leila's sister at the house she had rented high in the mountains, where the air was healthier for her own asthmatic son. Khaled took her mother there, intending to return to Beirut, but the village in the mountains came under Israeli air raids after Syrian forces fled. On June 12, Israeli tanks arrived. Her mother and sister were terrified that the notorious Leila Khaled would be recognized, but she reassured them that her face and figure had changed enough in the past decade that she wouldn't be spotted. "Besides," she said, "these are just soldiers, they are not intelligence, they don't know anything." The young children caused additional stress, her young nephew promising his aunt that "if they touch you I will kill them." "I told him, shut up, don't say anything," says Khaled, "but we were afraid because of the children."

Fayez, trapped in Beirut and with no means of getting in touch with his wife, was deeply upset. "Don't be afraid, we know Leila, she will manage," George Habash told him. He was right, but at times Khaled succeeded only by the skin of her teeth. After her sister discovered that the people she had rented the house from were Phalangists, Khaled "didn't sleep for about ten days" for fear that they would give her up to the Israelis. On one occasion a friend, who had hired another house in the village for a summer holiday planned before the war broke out, called Leila in while the Khaled family home was searched. Leila found a pistol, put a bullet in it and told herself, "If the Israelis come, I won't let them take me alive."

"For ten days, I was just watching the Israelis," says Khaled. "I saw the small children go to them and ask them questions about the tanks, and then the soldiers said 'go home now, we want to shell Beirut.' Imagine, seeing it like this, as if it was just out here on the street, and having to watch them shell Beirut." As she had suspected, she also had good reason to be afraid of loose tongues in the village, after some neighbors told her friends that they knew Leila Khaled was staying with them, and that she should leave for everyone's safety.

"My sister was about to have a breakdown and I was very much afraid," says Khaled. "In my mind I had accepted that if they came to arrest me I would kill myself. Eventually a friend from Tyre called Fatima, who was staying in the village with her family, came to me. She told me that their house had been searched by the Israelis and asked me to join them, so I moved there. After 12 days I wanted to go to Beirut with my mother. I took her and her mother's ID—she looked like me, she had the same eyes. And we went by car to Beirut. We were stopped by the Israelis, of course, but they didn't really look, just at the car, and I told them my mother was sick, which she really was of course. They said, 'nobody is going to Beirut, it's being shelled.' When it was them shelling it! But we told them we were taking my mother to the hospital, and we reached it, although nobody believed we would get there ... when I finally arrived in Beirut, our house was being used as a base for the fighters and Fayez was at the hospital. I went to see him, and he said, Dr George Habash told me you could manage."

To her annoyance, Khaled wasn't allowed to fight with the PLO commandos once it was known that she was pregnant. Instead, she worked with the General Union of Palestinian Women on the relief effort, helping the wounded and those displaced from the south and from areas under attack. Beirut was hideously crammed with refugees and fighters and was being shelled by tanks and from the air. Khaled was told that she was in danger of losing the baby. "I had to have these injections to stop the bleeding and the shelling was all the time, so we were running from one place to another," she recounts. August 1 was, she says, "terrible, the longest day." It was sweltering hot and the population was terrified. Rumors abounded that the attacks were coming from planes searching particularly for the PLO leadership, including Arafat, so when Khaled went into the shelters people tried to find others places to hide, thinking that she might draw fire towards them. "Fayez was at the hospital," she says again, "and all the schools and mosques had been turned into hospitals."

Finally, after defending Beirut for three months alongside the Lebanese national movement, the encircled Palestinian resistance agreed to leave the city. After a month of negotiations an agreement was reached: the leadership and fighters could leave, some by ship north up the Syrian coast or across the Mediterranean to Tunis and some by road to Syria. Under the terms of the agreement, a multinational peacekeeping force— American, Italian, and French—entered Beirut to protect the guerrillas' departure and to guarantee the safety of the Palestinian civilians left in the refugee camps, vulnerable now to attack from Phalangist and Israeli forces. This force carried out the first part of its mandate; tragically, it neglected the second.[14]

Leila and Fayez left by sea, travelling up the coast to Syria. They were taken first to a camp to be processed, but Khaled's comrades managed to have her transferred to a hotel because of her pregnancy. Then the Syrian authorities released the male fighters and Fayez joined her. Again, he was working in a hospital when on September 17, watching the news on television, Khaled saw reports of the massacres at the Sabra and Shatila refugee camps back in Beirut, carried out by the Phalangist militias under the auspices of the Israeli armed forces. Her screaming and shouting alerted the hotel staff, who knew that a woman from Lebanon was staying there, and when Fayez returned from work he learned that she had fainted and been taken to hospital.

Miserable and frustrated over events back in Lebanon and desperately worried for those they'd had to leave behind, the couple also faced the challenges of trying to re-establish some kind of life for themselves. Fayez had applied and been accepted for further medical training in Czechoslovakia, but the paperwork had been left in Beirut when they fled. The Czech embassy in Damascus had no record of his place, but they agreed to give the couple a visa to go to Czechoslovakia to try to resolve the issue. But the university there also claimed to have no record that he had been accepted and they had to return to Damascus. She flew back and he was meant to follow by train, because they only had enough money for one flight. But on her return, their comrades responded to the news by having a whip-round and sent Fayez a plane ticket.

Finding a home in Damascus proved equally difficult, so the couple had to stay in the hotel Khaled had been sent to when they first arrived. On December 5, she had a doctor's appointment in the makeshift hospital where Fayez and other Red Crescent volunteers were treating the wounded from Lebanon. The doctor, a friend of Fayez from his days in the Soviet Union, had agreed to see her briefly amongst the emergency patients.

"I remember it was windy, it was the first time it was windy," says Khaled, "and I was smoking and drinking coffee. The doctor came and saw me and she said, 'are you smoking?' Then she turned to Fayez and said, 'why do you let her smoke?' But he told her, 'we were in Beirut at the time of war and I kept giving her leaflets telling her that a pregnant woman shouldn't smoke. But then on the day when there was all the shelling, all day, I brought her two packets. We were not sure that we were going to get out alive.'"

Having heard this the doctor examined Khaled, who wasn't supposed to be due to give birth for another month. But without

hesitation she looked up and told her, "you're going to deliver."
Khaled insisted that she couldn't feel anything, and besides the
other doctors she had seen had calculated a due date of late
December or early January. "If it's the first day in your month, it
can be now," the doctor told her. "Now, walk, and tell me when
you feel that you want to go to the bathroom." Khaled didn't
even reach the end of the corridor before she realized the doctor
was right, and the next thing she knew she was lying down and
Fayez was being sent for clothes for the newborn baby. She was
in labor for just an hour and, says Khaled, "no one in that room
knew that I was giving birth. I didn't say a word, I just did what
she told me. My muscles were flexible from all the running from
one place to another, so it was easy, but I was afraid that I will
have a dead child, because he didn't finish his stay in my belly."

Her fears were unwarranted. The boy, called Bader as the
West Bank grandmother he would never meet had asked, cried
as he was slapped by the doctor. His mother cried too—for her
husband who hadn't returned from finding baby clothes, and for
their families who couldn't be there either. The doctor pointed
out that Khaled hadn't cried out at all during the birth, "but at
the end of it I felt the pain. I told her, I wanted to be happy at
this moment, with my husband, my family, my friends, but no
one is here and there are no clothes for the child. So what to
do? We took a sheet and wrapped him."

Leila Khaled might have hijacked airplanes and fought an
urban guerrilla war, but she was completely thrown by the
prospect of dealing with a new baby, especially living out of
a suitcase in a Damascus hotel. "I didn't know how to deal
with a child," she says. "It was really terrible." She tried to
breastfeed but couldn't, and the baby screamed for three days.
Two married comrades brought her to their home to help, but
none of them could comfort the crying child. Slowly she learnt
how to manage a newborn baby and finally, following a PFLP
order that its cadres should find homes in the already crowded
refugee camps, Fayez managed to find a house for the three of
them, in Yarmouk camp.

The next challenge for Khaled was accepting the fact that,
for now, she couldn't work. "That was also a new experience,"

she says. All around Damascus her PFLP comrades were having to re-organize their lives, rebuilding the structures and working relationships which had governed their work in Beirut. But, says Khaled, they also started to consider properly the need for kindergartens and nurseries. The leadership of the party might have paid lip service to women's issues in the past, but now that senior female members of its hierarchy had small children, problems of childcare and family commitments had become more immediately pressing. "When we joined the party we were young, we were not married," says Khaled. "But then the women cadres, they married and had children, so we thought about the need for these things. The first thing we decided is to have a nursery, so we asked the PFLP if we could start one to put our children in and of course they accepted, not only for the cadre women but also for the women in the camp. We arranged everything, the equipment, and they had sessions on how to deal with children, so we sent our children there so we could have time to go on with our work."

Existing as a woman in the PFLP, especially one with parental responsibilities, can be immensely difficult, as Khaled acknowledges. "I think from my experience and other people's experiences, for a woman in our society to be committed as a member of a party or struggling for liberation, the dangers that we face, it's difficult, and it's different from when you're single." Many women, she says, have left the movement because of the difficulty in balancing their roles, and divorces occur "because of the differences we find between how relationships should be and the practice of them." Julie Peteet confirms this pattern, noting that the resistance movements in Lebanon in the 1970s and early 1980s had a high drop-out rate amongst young women once they reached marriageable age. A period of activism was an accepted part of "girlhood," but once adult, women were expected to prioritize family responsibilities, domesticity and child-rearing. And those who remained in the movement, or who tried to push the political boundaries a little, found that efforts to raise "women's" issues were countered with accusations of being "bourgeois," and that over-ambitious young women found themselves being accused of promiscuity and improper behavior.[15]

Throughout the 1980s, therefore, Leila Khaled had to adapt to her new role, as a mother with two small children to care for—her second son Bashar followed soon after Bader—often on her own. "At that time Fayez was still in the Soviet Union, specializing," she says. The family were able to visit him occasionally, but with Khaled occupying a number of senior roles in the PFLP (including a seat on the Central Committee to which she had been elected in 1981) and, until 1985, in the General Union of Palestinian Women, it was hard work. "We went to visit him in 1985, at the end of December, and it was very difficult with two children and all my work. The Intifada broke out in the Occupied Territories in 1987 and we had a lot of activities to support them. And then there was the [1991] attack on Iraq and we were very, very busy. I asked my niece to come and live with me to help look after the children at least when I wasn't there. And I had to go to Palestinian National Council meetings in Algiers and other places, so for five years I was just running, running all the time."

Even so, Khaled recognizes that she has been lucky in her second marriage. "I depended very much on my husband," she says. "Although he was a member of the PFLP before we met he still gets stressed about it, about my travelling so much. It took us a long time to cope. But other women face such problems with their families, especially with the men. Even single women, if it's not the father it's the brothers, if it's not the brothers, it's the uncle."

As their children grew up, Leila Khaled and other senior women in the PFLP continued to influence the party's attitudes and structures with their own direct experiences. Progressive theories on gender relations were, apparently, no substitute for the day-to-day challenges facing the women with significant roles in the movement. As Khaled describes it, "all those years, until 1982 to 1992, I was based in Syria. I had to balance work and the children. It was the same for other women comrades, so we began to discuss the issue of women comrades who became mothers in the party, that all the women are taking care of children but what about the men?! So we took a decision that all comrades are responsible for caring for the children. Also, the meetings used to go on until 11 or 12 at night, and we took a decision that mothers should not have to sit up like this, so late. And actually this was met with appreciation from the leadership, including people like Dr George Habash and Abu Ali Mustafa, who supported us. The movement had to respond to the realities of life. Before, I was single, I could go everywhere, and this was the same for other women comrades, but now I'm responsible for other human beings, especially when my husband wasn't there to help."

5

Revolutionary Women

Leila Khaled's position as a specifically *female* icon of the Palestinian struggle has always been an ambiguous one. As one young Palestinian woman activist put it, "I realized that even though I was raised to idolize the women revolutionary fighters, I was never meant to become like them. I was meant to get married, have kids, be a good wife and support my husband. I was taught that these women were important components of the Palestinian resistance, but I was not meant to become one of them because that would mean I was not a 'good Arab woman.'"[1]

Both Palestinian and Western feminist commentators have highlighted the chasm between the respect given to individual high-profile women militants such as Khaled, and the multiple oppressions which face women in a patriarchal society which is also a largely refugee community and/or one living under military occupation. For "ordinary" women activists in many Palestinian communities, both in the diaspora or in the West Bank and Gaza, their activism has resulted in pressure or even rejection from family members or their immediate community who want to see them return to a more "respectable" female role.[2] In common with most other national struggles, Palestinian nationalist discourse is highly gendered, referring in official documents, speeches, and other texts to the "rape" of the "mother" country and featuring art and poetry which depicts Palestine as a female entity to be protected from masculine Zionist aggression. Although women are valued in this language, they remain passive or are confined to stereotypical roles.[3] And although a discourse of self-criticism amongst Palestinian leaders and intellectuals of the 1970s and '80s emphasized the need for Palestinian society to "modernize"—including in its attitudes to women[4]—this has not always translated into change on the ground.

Women have been involved in Palestinian national movements since at least the early twentieth century.[5] Women participated in the demonstrations and campaigns against the Balfour Declaration of 1917 and Zionist immigration onto land sold by absentee Ottoman landlords.[6] During the 1936 Palestinian rebellion women delivered weapons, food, and water to the (male) fighters and organized support for destitute families, especially those of men imprisoned by the British Mandate authorities. A female activist interviewed by Palestinian writer Soraya Antonius in the 1970s recalled that she "had some training with a rifle but I never fought. Mainly we prepared food and took it to the fighters because the men couldn't move around as freely as we could, and we acted as couriers and collected money for the movement." The same woman also described practicing how to shoot during the 1947–48 war.[7] And in the Nakba of 1948 women took part both in organizing relief where they could, and in a very few cases—such as that of Helwa Zaidan, who picked up her son's weapons after he and her husband were killed in front of her—in the fighting itself.[8]

Immediately after the Nakba, the majority of Palestinian women were concerned with their own survival and women's public activity declined. It re-emerged in the 1950s and '60s, primarily in women's associations and charities run by middle-class women or, by the late 1960s, through women's organizations allied to and often largely governed by the main political factions.[9] From the late 1970s a feminist women's movement developed, although it remained a minority and again was largely confined to the middle classes;[10] the bulk of women's political activity was still associated with the nationalist movement or charitable activities around children or family support rather than addressing issues relating to their specific position as women.[11]

Nevertheless, says anthropologist Julie Peteet, Palestinian women in Lebanon especially "joined all spheres of the resistance. Few attained leadership positions and most were concentrated in the social services sector. Nevertheless, women were now more than wives and mothers: they were fighters, leaders, workers, students, activists, cadres and martyrs. The social practices associated with these categories of activism were accompanied by a new sense of identity and extra-domestic aspirations."[12] Women participated in operations both on Israeli territory and internationally and at times, although not always, their achievements were recognized by the largely male political leaderships. Soraya Antonius described in 1979 how, in 1967,

> when the Resistance movement began in Jordan, and in 1969, when it opened up the camps in Lebanon, a new idea began, slowly, to percolate: that women constitute half the available manpower resource, one that a small, embattled nation cannot afford to waste. Women began to participate, publicly, in every crisis, from Wahdat camp in the 1970 Amman battles to the latest Israeli invasion in South Lebanon.[13]

And Bassam Abu-Sharif, former PFLP spokesman turned Arafat ally, noted of the First Intifada: "The Israeli security forces, swamped, tried rounding up all the young men and sending them to prison camps in the Negev desert. But the ... women's committees simply took over, leading the revolution successfully for more than three months."[14]

But the extent to which women who prioritize national struggle over a feminist agenda are betraying both their sisters and themselves is something which still provokes heated and at times vitriolic debate. Nationalism, conflict, and national liberation struggles do not intersect with gender in any simple way. As Wenona Giles puts it in *Feminists Under Fire*:

> War is an ambivalent process for women. While on the one hand they suffer acutely from its violence, on the other, those living in traditional patriarchal societies may find that war is a time of release from the constricting hierarchies of peacetime existence. But such a gain can rarely be sustained in the aftermath of war. Different kinds of wars permit different kinds of female participation, and women's lives are affected in a variety of ways by the resolution of war...[15]

Neloufer de Mel continues this conversation in a later section of the same book by turning to an analysis of women in the military. She argues that the times when a Tamil woman might feel most empowered through armed battle, are in fact times when a woman's freedom is controlled through the repression of her sexuality and gendered identity *as a woman*. "Although an armed woman warrior might enjoy a degree of liberty, having transcended the prescribed female role, her freedom is diminished through the patriarchal enforcement of discipline."[16] Some feminist writers talk about women who prioritize national liberation as if they are fooled by patriarchal discourse or the victims of iron restrictions which prevent them from making alternative choices.[17] Even Palestinian women's rights activists and scholars, many of whom have been closely involved in the struggle for their people's rights, differ on this issue.[18]

The ambiguity surrounding Leila Khaled as an icon of women's liberation starts with her own involvement in the Palestinian women's movement. In short, she didn't really want to be involved in it at all.

In the early 1970s, after her return from British captivity and as she was working with George Hajjar on her autobiography and as a militant in the camps in Lebanon, George Habash also asked Khaled to become one of the PFLP's representatives in the General Union of Palestinian Women, one of the PLO's "mass organizations" which at the time was supposed to be an umbrella body for all Palestinian women, those from any of the PLO factions or those affiliated to none.

Khaled, however, was extremely reluctant. "I refused," she says. "I told them, 'I'm a fighter, I want to hold arms.' They said, 'you are also a woman, you have also to fight for the rights of women.' I told them, 'I can't do that, it's a mission and it's very difficult and I don't like it.'" With the benefit of hindsight, she says of her twenty-something self: "some of the women comrades, I maybe was one of them, thought that we wanted to prove that we could do the same things as men. So we dressed like men, we cut our hair short like men, and we showed that we could bear arms. We didn't think about women. We didn't think it was our business."

Her reasoning, though, highlights one of the classic debates about how women's position should be advanced in society— whether by highlighting specific challenges that women encounter in society and working to address them, or by integrating women in men's roles to "prove" that they can be "equal" by doing the same things with equal success, or by building a theoretically more egalitarian society in which *all* oppressions, including those based on sex and gender, are diminished.

Khaled, in her mid twenties and with two airplane hijackings under her belt, very much subscribed to the second viewpoint. "I had the idea that women in our society are looked upon as second-class citizens," she says. "Those who joined the revolution, including myself, wanted to prove that we can be equal in missions and in practice with men. The highest rank for us was to bear arms, so we just wanted to prove ourselves in their field like this." But according to Khaled, George Habash himself called her to a meeting and said "'as a woman you have to fight for the rights of women, you have to be the voice of women.' OK, I had to accept, but with not very much confidence."

Almost 40 years later, Khaled still insists that the example of women who participated in the armed struggle has had a significant impact for all Palestinian women. "In practice, I think we have achieved many achievements for women in that we held arms because it convinced men that women can do the same as men, because to use arms is politics in practice. This is what I understand about armed struggle."

But, she acknowledges perhaps more than she might have in her younger years as a commando: "Women as human beings—we are not speaking about women as different from men biologically—in our case I think we are under complicated oppression. We are under occupation, and in that we are equal in oppression with men. We are refugees, also we are equal with men in this. At the same time, there is social oppression and it's strong, so women when they bear arms, they are trying to participate in the national struggle and also in the social struggle."

One of Khaled's early challenges was negotiating the complex internal politics of the GUPW conference in 1974. This was the Union's second conference; the first, held in Jerusalem in 1967, had been met by the Israeli authorities with arrests and deportations. Those arrested included the Union's President,

Issam Abdel Hadi, a veteran campaigner who was released without charge.

The 1974 conference, held in Lebanon, was riven by factional disputes between the left and right wings of the Palestinian national liberation movement. The scheduled three days extended to seven and, according to Khaled, events were being watched closely even by Yasser Arafat, who was visiting Cuba.

"Arafat came directly from Cuba to the place where we were holding the conference," Khaled recalls. The Union had been discussing Fatah's proposal for a "provisional solution" which would shift the emphasis of the PLO from armed struggle to a political resolution of the issue of Palestine. According to Amal Kawar:

> Inside the Women's Union, Fateh's Abu Khadra led the pro group with the argument that the international and regional power balance had changed in favor of Israel after its rapprochement with Egypt. Popular Front's Leila Khaled led the opposition, arguing that this was a drastic departure from the PLO Charter and that armed struggle was the only chip left in the hands of the Palestinians to use against Israel ... Arafat scored a qualified victory when the Women's Union passed a compromise resolution. The women supported the Provisional Solution but also included a qualification that supported all decisions of the National Council—which meant supporting the 1968 National Charter and the armed struggle. Both Khaled and Abdel Hadi, however, had remained opposed. The compromise was face-saving for Arafat and his followers, but it left him unhappy with the renegades within his own faction.[19]

Khaled's recollection is that "He wanted us to change the declaration we had agreed at the end of the conference, and we refused, and he was very furious. But there were 150 women delegates there, some of them representing countries, not just NGOs, so we refused [to change it] even though he was very angry."

In 1975 the Lebanese civil war started in earnest, but it was also the United Nations Year of Women. "So," says Khaled, "we were in a place where there was a civil war; at the same time as a Union we have to carry out our program, our plans, to be part of that Year. And the first thing the UN specified was that in every country there should be a national committee to deal with the issues in that country, to promote and empower women in that society. It was difficult for us because we were not a 'country,' by 1974 the PLO was recognized in the UN as an observer, so we were dealt with in the same way as the ANC and SWAPO, as a liberation movement."

The General Union embarked on its plans for the Year of Women, trying to take advantage of interludes in the fighting to implement the program. And, despite her initial skepticism about being ordered to join the Union, Khaled found that the work she had to do was both fulfilling and educational. "I had to train other women in the camps because we had to defend ourselves and to mobilize," she says, "so I had to go from one house to another in the camps, and this experience was a great one for me, I learned a lot from the people, how to be modest. I began to realize the problems that women suffer from, not only that they are refugees, we are all refugees and in the camps people are living in a difficult situation, but at the same time I began to listen more to the problems of women. This gave me another reason to play a role in the union, not as a representative of PFLP but as a woman, to work out how to solve the problems of women. This combination was a big experience for me. I also learnt about the life of women in villages as well as in the refugee camps, where it's accepted that a woman goes to work to earn money for the family, but she cannot choose her partner, and that's a problem. She's exploited by the extended family to earn money, but she's not free to choose her own political position, she has to be like her brother or her husband. It's a big problem."

These experiences were something which Khaled took to the other PFLP and PLO positions she was elected to, including her seat on the Palestinian National Council (PNC). "We began to discuss women's issues in 1979, to discuss them as issues in the revolution itself," she says. "Although we had the General Union and women's organizations and they work on women's issues we didn't deal with them in the [PFLP] party itself. So we began to transfer our ideas—are women represented in the PLO? In the PNC? There were women in these but no woman had reached the Executive Committee, and we raised this all the time in the PNC. International Women's Day, the 8th of March, wasn't recognized by the movement, so we started that in 1979 and not just with women, we invited the leaders from the different factions to come and discuss women's issues."

THE INTERNATIONAL STAGE

Far from the poverty of the refugee camps in Lebanon, the General Union of Palestinian Women was also taking part in the international women's gatherings of the 1970s. In June 1975, the first World Conference on Women was held by the UN in Mexico, and in the revolutionary spirit of the time passed a motion condemning Zionism as racism. The same motion was passed by the UN General Assembly in 1978.[20] But even at conferences in socialist countries which had supported the Palestinian cause since the 1950s, Khaled says they encountered increasing pressure "not to mention Zionism" from Soviet delegations and from the President of the Women's International Democratic Federation, Frieda Braun. "She said, as long as it's mentioned in the UN, we don't have to mention it again. So for issues dealing with women, all of us from different countries, we didn't have any conflict. But about political issues, we had conflicts."

But if the women she had met in the Lebanese refugee camps had taught Leila Khaled about her own people, attending international conferences also opened her eyes to issues she'd never dreamt of. "In a session in one of the conferences," Khaled recounts, "a woman asked to speak, and she declared herself a representative for lesbians. And for me, I said, 'what is that?' It's beyond our thinking. And from the beginning, she said: 'those men on the platform (because there were two men, and one of them was a priest)—those men are our enemies.' She told them to step down from the platform and leave. So we left as well, and so did the other [panelists], so she stayed on the platform making her speech and recording it. Afterwards, I was going round and asking 'what does that mean?' For myself, I hadn't any idea about it."

It wasn't the first time that Palestinian sexual conservatism had clashed with the liberal mores of the 1970s. In 1969, according to Khaled, she had been present when a group of foreign students attending the General Union of Palestinian Students conference paid a visit to a PFLP training camp, probably in Jordan, although she says she can't definitely remember. "One of the women said to us, 'how do you deal with sexual issues?' We didn't think of it, even, and we certainly didn't discuss it. So we said, 'this is not an issue to be discussed.' And they asked us, 'how do you live? How do you have relationships?' And we said, we don't. In the camp, the tents for the men are apart from the tents for the women. We don't want our people to prevent their women coming to the camps, so we had to pay attention to the traditions of society. At the same time we can change by education society's ideas, but slowly, gradually."

"That was the first time we discussed this issue, and one of the students said, 'yes, we have sexual relations with men,' and of course it was without marriage, and we said how? It's not allowed. One of our women said, 'no no no, don't listen to Leila,' because I said we don't discuss such issues, and she wanted to show that because we are of the left, we are progressive and all issues are decided in our party, but I said 'no, this is something we don't discuss.'"[21]

International conferences didn't just introduce Leila Khaled to novel sexual ideas. They also forced her to meet with her Israeli enemies in an environment which wasn't an airplane hijacking or a military confrontation—and in some cases to accept that they might even be her allies. At the same conference where Khaled's delegation walked out on the lesbian speaker, the Palestinians also had to deal with the prospect of encountering a group from Maki, the Israeli Communist Party, which also included Palestinian citizens of Israel.

"We had decided that we won't have anything to do with them," says Khaled. "Our common friends, especially the Soviets, were asking us, why don't you speak with them? We said, we don't speak with people who are occupying our houses.

Even the Palestinians, they are representing Israelis, so we don't speak to them." But in the busy environment of an international conference, it wasn't always possible to avoid everyone: "I was going to a plenary session, and a man and a woman were standing outside," Khaled recounts, "I knew the man, he was a Soviet writer, and he said to me 'Hi Leila, how are you? Come over.' He was speaking in Arabic. And the woman came and hugged me, and I realized that her accent was not Arabic. She spoke Arabic, but when a foreigner speaks Arabic, the accent is very noticeable. I asked her, 'are you Soviet?' And my friend said to me, 'don't you know her?' I said 'no, who are you?' And he said, 'this is Felicia Langer, the Israeli lawyer who defends all the Palestinian prisoners in Israeli jails.' And I said, 'OK, nice meeting you,' and left. I was shaking. One of the members of our groups asked what was wrong with me, and ... the tears came. I said, 'Imagine! Felicia Langer hugged me!'"

But, says Khaled, the PFLP delegation listened to Langer speak in a later session and watched her take letter after letter from her handbag and read from them the accounts of Palestinian women in Israeli jails and of the torture they endured, "she spoke about the racist state in Israel," Khaled remembers. "We were astonished, and we had a meeting as a delegation and asked ourselves, why have we taken this attitude? This woman speaks like us."

In 1980 Copenhagen hosted the second big United Nations women's conference, half way through its Decade for Women. Khaled was there as part of a wider PLO delegation because the PLO, with UN observer status, was permitted to attend and discuss such events, but not to vote in them. But for Khaled her participation in the event was overshadowed by death threats against her and reports that the Israeli government was seeking her extradition from Denmark.[22] Apparently she could cope with the daily threat of life on the front line of a bloody war zone, but to be out of her element, in an environment she couldn't evaluate, was harder to handle. "Every day I received threatening letters," she says. "Our delegation was afraid, because some of the letters said 'we will kill you here. We will not let you go out from Denmark,' and they were criticizing the government for letting me come to Denmark and so on, and for not sending me to Israel. I had to live in a different way from our delegation."

Although Khaled had attended many international conferences during the 1970s, mainly women's gatherings but sometimes on other issues, many of these had been in the socialist countries and she hadn't attracted much attention at them from the Western press or Western feminists. At Copenhagen, she "re-emerged," as some rather arrogantly put it, and not all of them liked what they saw.

The tension between nationalism and feminism seemed, for some, to be embodied in Leila Khaled, and she attracted considerable hostility from the likes of Robin Morgan, a veteran of the late 1960s US women's movement and, perhaps ironically given some of the vitriol she directed at Khaled, editor of *Sisterhood is Global*. But in her analysis of the gendering and sexuality of terrorism, in which one of her main theses is that women who participate in terrorist acts generally do so as the pawns of men or as some kind of surrogate male themselves, she has this to say about Khaled:

> The [PLO] men, who headed the delegation even though this was a women's conference, were furious that so much attention was paid to a woman. The women expressed irritation (off-stage and unofficially in private conversations) because Khaled never spoke about *women*. But her reasons came out a year later in an interview with a German feminist newspaper. She displayed the elite disdain for which PFLP commandos are notorious—a contempt for the fedayeen who make lowly border raids on Israeli kibbutzim—compounded with a double message about being female: "when I speak at an international conference, as in Copenhagen, I represent Palestinians, not women ... although in Arab society to be married and have children is very important, in my case nobody wonders about it. A woman who fights politically is respected ... the organisers and organisations would not take us seriously if we were to begin speaking about it [women's rights]. They would say we wish to be like European women ... and they would reject us. So we try to say that honour means more than virginity, that there is honour in recovering our homeland."... She has not survived being female. It's clear in the interview: even for the unattached woman, the gestures of obeisance, the protestations of

denial, must be made. The woman who rebels via the male mode can do
so only to the point where her own rebellion might begin.[23]

(It should perhaps be noted that other writers on the subject do
not corroborate Morgan's claim that the Palestinian delegation
was headed by men; according to Amal Kawar, it was led by
Fatah's Mai Sayigh and Jihan Helou. GUPW President Issam
Abdel Hadi attended part of the conference but left due to
ill-health.[24])

British journalist Jill Tweedie was less scathing than Morgan,
but not by much. She seems to have strongly resented not being
able to get an interview with Khaled, and roundly criticized
the "united and determinedly anonymous phalanx" of the PLO
delegation which, in contrast to Morgan, she suggests was all
female. But she concurs with Morgan's account of the difficulties
of getting Khaled, or any of the other Palestinian women, to talk
about women per se, although Tweedie does describe managing
to grab a brief interview—"A polite euphemism for forcibly
pinning her down for four minutes, using my back as a shield
against the trampling buffalo herd behind her—I learned that
Miss Khaled has always been alive and well and living in Beirut.
She is unmarried and, as a member of the Union of Palestinian
Women, devotes her days to working in the Palestinian refugee
camps of the Lebanon, helping women in literacy classes and
looking after orphaned Palestinian children." Tweedie goes
on to say that "Her work over the past ten years differs in
no essential way from her youthful hijacking exploits—it is
all done to further the cause of the Palestinian homeland."
And, apparently inevitably, she comments on Khaled's "fatal
Garboesque appeal."[25]

FEMINISM AND NATIONALISM

Khaled's own position on the question of feminism versus
nationalism is clear. Firstly, she states that: "some researchers
in our region have said that women should confront inequalities

with men and social oppression before the national question. This is a very serious issue, and we had big discussions about it. The question for me is, which is the most direct oppression? It's the occupation. For men and women, children and elderly, it's the same. We said, who are the first oppressors of the Palestinians? It's the Occupation."

But she also cites pragmatic reasons for her position, suggesting that under the conditions which have existed in the West Bank and Gaza since 1967, any social activist—whether working directly against the Occupation or not—is liable to arrest. "They said no," she recounts, "first we have to change society? And we said, you're not going to win that because you yourself will be taken to prison. Now which is more dangerous? The one who puts you in prison or your father who will not allow you to choose your partner? The more dangerous one is that which endangers your life, your family's life, it's comprehensive."

Khaled also, however, doesn't completely agree with those who believe that total equality for women will be achieved through socialism. "We believe that the struggle can achieve some rights for us," she says, "but it doesn't always go in parallel. In any society you have an inheritance of culture and traditions and you can't just change that through laws and politics, you need generations to change it gradually. Politically you can change, economically you can change more easily, but these are questions of culture and it depends on education. We understand that, when women gain their rights it means that men are losing their privileges and their authority."

Linda Clair, a Jewish Palestine solidarity activist from the UK who has been friends with Khaled since meeting her at a conference in Libya in 1988, also suggested that "generally I don't think people who come down on the feminism side of the argument have direct experience of struggle," although she admits that there are some Palestinian feminists who would reject that line. Aitemad Muhanna, a former PFLP activist from Gaza, for instance, notes of her experience of being physically attacked by Hamas activists for not wearing the veil that "My active commitment to national resistance and mass mobilization counted for nothing when it came to the veil and protection by my leftist party and its members ... I started to think about my identity as a woman, and how it was obscured by my identity as a nationalist leftist subject. I could no longer take for granted the link between national liberation and individuals'/women's freedom."[26] And as early as 1979 Palestinian poet and activist Mai Sayigh described how "Abu Ammar [Yasser Arafat] thinks women should go to the bases and fight and live there, but he doesn't understand that we have difficulty just getting women to leave their homes alone in broad daylight. One can't jump several stages just like that, it's as mistaken an idea as keeping women locked up at home. If she goes to the bases she'll be considered a prostitute. I remember when we started going to the camps in Jordan, in 1967–68, all the men used to greet us by lining the streets and chanting, ironically, 'Here come the feda'iya.'"[27] The GUPW had to "hew a road through rock" to change the position of women in Palestinian society, Sayigh went on to say. According to a grassroots activist, "Fatmeh," from a Palestinian refugee camp in Lebanon, it was only the siege of Tel al-Za'atar camp in 1976 and the sense of extreme threat to the entire community that convinced some men that women had a place on the front line. "[N]o one stopped his daughter because everybody felt threatened by the danger and the neighbors couldn't gossip because all the women—mothers, daughters, wives and sisters—all worked."[28]

Leila Khaled has seen major change over her four decades in the Popular Front. The party has always, claims Khalil Meqdisi, been ahead of other factions in recruiting and promoting women, citing cases such as Shadiah Abu Ghazaleh, a PFLP military commander from Nablus who was the first female Palestinian "martyr" of the resurgent resistance of the 1960s. Khaled used her name as a nom de guerre on her own 1969 mission.

Even so, says Khaled, "the first time I led a group of fighters, in Lebanon, one of the men said 'you can't lead us' and some of them refused. The chief of the military section told them, 'it's a war, you can't choose who you serve under, you don't discuss, you obey orders.' For me, though, it was easier than for other women comrades because after the hijackings I was known, but for some of the other women officers they would say, 'we are ready to die—but not in the leadership of a woman.' Even in wartime we used to have to go and waste time discussing it. But there were four of us women officers and so the men began to know us and to trust us more. But this took 40 years. During the struggle we could break many old ideas and many traditions in society and in the party, but it was very difficult, for the party and for us. Some women thought in the 1970s that we have to be equal even in our houses—that if I wash the dishes he has to wash the dishes too. This is difficult. Again, we had to discuss it, we had to change it gradually, not radically. Some people were saying: we have to be gradual in talking about these things, or the male members will start being afraid of the party itself."

In this mural, located in the West Bank city of Beit Sahur, Khaled's image appears alongside those of assassinated PFLP writer Ghassan Kanafani (also shown) and the three secretaries-general of the PFLP: George Habash, Abu Ali Mustafa and Ahmad Sa'adat (Sarah Irving).

Under internal pressure from its own women cadres and from events in the wider world—principally the recognition that women in the Occupied Territories were being imprisoned and killed, but that the issues they faced in the struggle were different from those confronting male activists—the PFLP began to include gender issues in educational programs throughout the party's ranks, commissioning information on the role of women in the party. "That was important," says Khaled, "because theoretically any party can say it has equality between men and women but in the PFLP it's different, because of the way people have to prove themselves as members, so it needs to think about the issues for women to be nominated to higher ranks."

WOMEN IN THE PFLP

The PFLP, as a Marxist revolutionary organization drawing inspiration from the ideas of figures like Che Guevara and Fidel Castro,[29] had, like its forerunner the Arab Nationalist Movement, instituted a strict internal regimen of duties and responsibilities.[30] As we've already seen, members were required to seek the leadership's approval for major life decisions like marriage and to prove their commitment through activity before being admitted to full membership. This has meant that the PFLP's political clout has always been greater than its formal membership. The latter has never been made public for obvious security reasons, but some commentators place it at a few thousand or, more recently, in the high hundreds.[31] It was these strict internal regulations that the PFLP woman had to influence and, says Khaled, it was at times a struggle. "Fatah, it's a petit-bourgeois movement and more people join it because it is more open to different political ideas. In the PFLP, we have a lot of commitments, it's not organized the same way, and as Marxists, having Marxist ideas, we adopted a lot of new ways. We are practicing our ideas about how women and men work together equally in the struggle, but we also have big arguments about that."

And at the grassroots level, rather than in the higher echelons and formal membership of the factions, women's roles were even more contested. A Palestinian militant from Nahr al-Bared camp in Lebanon told Rosemary Sayigh in the 1970s that "the circle of fear was over, and now there was an active movement in the camp. For the first time in our history women took their right role, and there was military training for girls as well as boys. We felt we had regained our identity, not just as Palestinians, but as human beings."[32] But others were less sanguine about the opening up of women's roles in the Palestinian resistance. According to one woman militant who grew up in the refugee camps in Lebanon and was interviewed by Sayigh in the 1970s:

> Up to now the Revolution hasn't given woman her authentic role. The Revolution still understands the role of women in a way that doesn't allow her to get free from her cage ... the majority of our women up to now are not able to struggle against their families so as to share in political activity ... I know people who are in responsible positions in the Revolution, and who claim that they are real revolutionaries, but who still do not allow their wives and daughters to take part in the Revolution.[33]

Leila Khaled acknowledges that the job is far from finished. "Men in the PFLP, not all of them are convinced that a woman can do it. It takes time to educate, but women proved also by practice that they can lead." The first women were, she says, elected to the PFLP's Central Committee at its third conference in 1972 and numbers here and in the Politburo have slowly increased. There have been three women in the PFLP Politburo since the sixth conference in 2000, says Khalil Meqdisi—Leila Khaled, Khalida Jarrar, and Mariam Abu Dagga. Increasing women's representation by election is also, Khaled points out, a slow process, especially as the PFLP hasn't held a conference since 2000 because of the situation in the West Bank and Gaza and the imprisonment of its current General Secretary, Ahmad Sa'adat, in Israel.

Not all the changes demanded by women in the PFLP fell on sympathetic ears. When, at the party's fourth conference in 1981, women from within the movement approached the leadership with a proposal to ban polygamy amongst the PFLP membership, they were challenged by comrades who asked them, "do we have members in the PFLP who are married twice?" "And we said, maybe one or two," says Khaled. The party apparently feared that, by addressing what men within it saw as a marginal issue rather than a situation of widespread oppression of women within the movement, it would stir up controversy and possible opposition to the PFLP for rejecting a direct Islamic religious ruling, "so we don't mention it in our documents now," says Khaled. "We discuss it on a case by case basis, but it is not an official position of the party, because our documents, our policies, are open to the masses and if we wrote it in them it would be known. So we had to accept that."

And, although she cites the increase in the number of women in senior PFLP positions, Khaled also acknowledges that the PLO has never followed suit. "We discussed these things with the others, the Fatah women, but I don't think we could have a document for the PLO itself, as the PLO, dealing with women's vision, because the women there are elected from the different parties and factions, not as women, and they have many different views. And on the question of why we didn't reach the leadership of the PLO? We need more women to be decision makers, to reach the higher positions, and in the PLO that hasn't happened yet. We discussed it but we have never reached a policy, a document, on how we see our liberation socially, its connection with the national struggle. We need to know more about this, there is lots written about women's issues but we need to know more about history, about women in our history."

According to calculations made by Amal Kawar in the mid 1990s, of the main PLO factions, women fared best in the DFLP, where they made up 28 percent of the membership, 17 percent of the Central Committee and 13 percent of the Political Bureau. In the PFLP, they represented 15 percent of the cadre and held 5 percent of Central Committee seats and none of those in the Political Bureau (in 2008 this changed, with Leila Khaled, Khalida Jarrar, and Mariam Abu Dagga all on the Political Bureau). The poorest showing came from Fatah, where women made up just 7 percent of delegates to the organization's Fourth Congress in

1980; the Fifth Congress elected six women—up from one—to the 80-member Revolutionary Council.[34] Within the PNC, Kawar later noted that the small number of women standing meant that women were seriously under-represented, and that practices such as quotas for other groups, such as Christian Palestinians, and deals made to reinforce Fatah's power base made it especially difficult for women to get onto its electoral slate. In 1996, the PFLP introduced gender quotas for its Sixth Congress but, says Kawar, "a leading female member of the secretive Popular Front noted her surprise at discovering how much tribalism dominated the leadership ranks, as evident by the fact that male leaders chose their female relatives for certain women's leadership roles."[35] Leila Khaled, however, denies that this statement "reflects reality."

Leila Khaled stresses the need for a greater understanding of the situation of Palestinian women, of the struggles they face, the effects of long-term refugee existence or of military occupation, and of why they have, in her eyes, lost ground after the progress they made in the 1970s and 1980s. "I think we have to have an in-depth study now about why women have gone backwards in our society," she says. "The whole situation is difficult. We have all the theory, now we need to be able to discuss the realities. And also, not just women. We need to know the impact of occupation on our children and what the television and the curriculum in school and all these things do to what they think. We need to know what changes happen to people living in a society under military occupation or in exile."

The relationship within the General Union between women from the different factions had sometimes been uneasy, but in the wake of the 1982 exodus from Beirut, dispersal and political disagreements divided the Union further. Most members of the GUPW leadership who were linked to Fatah headed for Tunisia rather than to Damascus, where the left-wing factions largely based themselves. After PLO Chairman Yasser Arafat's visit to Egypt in 1985, the relations between Syria and Fatah deteriorated;[36] Arafat arranged for the Palestinian National Council to meet in Amman, and Fatah prohibited the General Union of Palestinian Women from working in Syria. The PFLP elected to boycott the PNC over the many political disagreements it had with Arafat at the time, although mainly over the issue of dialogue with Israel. The GUPW decided to hold its conference, the first since it had moved to Tunisia, in Amman as well. So the PFLP and other PLO factions boycotted that too.

While its relations with the GUPW remained patchy, the PFLP worked on women's issues via its Palestinian Popular Women's Committees. During the 1970s, younger women of the activist generation formed the Committees to carry out political education and campaigning alongside the charitable work of the established women's movement in the Occupied Territories. By the early 1980s, however, these had split into four separate organizations, reflecting the different factions.[37] In 1981 the PFLP's Union of Palestinian Popular Women's Committees (PWC) was founded, to "struggle to empower Palestinian women and develop their circumstances to achieve real equality between men and women as well as equity among all social classes ... The [PWC], on the other hand, considers itself part of the Palestinian national movement that struggles against the Israeli illegal occupation to achieve national independence."[38] As well as political activities, the Committees supported income-generation cooperatives and social programs such as daycare centers. Leila Khaled was elected president in 1986, while she was still living in Yarmouk refugee camp.[39]

Answering charges that the PFLP's group duplicated or sought to challenge the role of the GUPW, "We said that the General Union had stopped working in Syria because Fatah and Syria are not on good terms, so we had to do something here, so this is our mass organization here," Khaled claims. The organization was, she insists, intended to be one of the member organizations under the umbrella of the GUPW, not a substitute for it, and that initial plans to call it the Palestinian Women's Organization were changed so as not to anger the GUPW leadership. "The aim of this was to organize women who may or may not be party members in the national and social struggle," says Khaled. Overall, the committees have been a significant organizing tool for left-oriented women, especially during the Intifadas in the West Bank and Gaza, where many activists within them have been targeted for arrest and detention by the Israeli security forces.[40] Although the membership of the committees was not made public, during the mid 1990s they claimed to have 5–6,000 activists, many of them amongst students.[41]

Despite the PFLP's rejection of the Oslo Accords, in 1996 the West Bank/Gaza section of the PWC did join the Women's Affairs Technical Committee (WATC), founded in 1994 as part of the Ministry of Planning, which worked to further women's rights in the new Oslo-era Occupied Territories. In its own words, the WATC's purpose was to "be part of the organization and infrastructure building of a future Palestinian state, to integrate gender into all preparatory work in support of the peace process, and to build state institutions in a manner that would fulfill the Declaration of Independence (1988) which affirms the principle of equality among Palestinians regardless of sex, religion or race." Although the PFLP remained opposed to the Oslo process, Giacaman and Johnson believe that, "In part, the PWC was convinced by the WATC's consistent policy of 'women's interests first' and its non-governmental character. In addition, the PWC, while holding real interest in developing women's issues, had been considerably weakened internally and needed to become a 'player' in the new terrain of women's advocacy and lobbying to reconstitute itself and have access to resources, whether material or political."[42]

6
Moving to Jordan and Returning to Palestine

In 1992, Leila Khaled and her husband decided to leave Damascus and move to Amman in Jordan, but the ambiguous legal positions of Palestinian refugees meant that there was nothing simple about the family's decision to relocate. Her husband, Fayez, having acquired his medical degree in physiotherapy and acupuncture, wanted to establish a clinic. The main problem facing the family was getting a passport for him and their children. Fayez went to Jordan to get his passport which had been revoked by the authorities, as Jordan had just opened the door for those who wished to return to the country.

He was granted a temporary passport by the Jordanian authorities. Immigration officials then decided that he could bring the children to live with him but—harking back to the turmoil of 1970—they refused to give permission for Khaled to join them. Bader and Bashar had only their birth certificate from the hospital in Syria where they were born, which identified Leila Khaled as their mother. Eventually the Jordanians agreed to interview Leila with a view to admitting her to live with her family, but it took two years for her and her sons to obtain passports. Once the family had permission to remain in Jordan, they also faced the exhausting task of establishing a new home.

"We arrived in 1992 and it was really difficult to find a house, because it was just after all the Palestinians were driven out of Kuwait because of the first Gulf War," recalls Khaled. "Fayez had just established his clinic so we had to take out loans from the bank, and we had to hire a furnished apartment which is very expensive here. Then we had to find a school for the children and the problem then was that in Syria they don't teach children English from the first grade, they teach it from the fifth grade and so they were behind and that was very difficult. For one year I couldn't do anything here, just coming from one country to another, searching for a house, so I didn't have any political activity."

The hardships faced by the Khaled family didn't stop with Leila's immediate domestic problems. In September 1991 her youngest brother, only in his early thirties, died after a year-long illness, and six months later the family lost another brother. "After all this I began to face sadness and grief" admits Khaled. "But it's not in my hands."

Although Leila Khaled, Fayez, and their family have settled, apparently happily, in Amman, growing up with her as a mother has not always been easy for her children. "I brought my children up to have their own personalities," she says. "They have their father's name and not their mother's, and all the time they were children I told them, 'don't say I'm your mother in front of the other children at school.' It wasn't that my sons are not proud of me or don't love me, but I wanted them to grow up to be their own personalities, to speak to people as themselves. Only lately have some of their friends from when they were at high school found out that I'm their mother and at university as well they don't talk about it."

"I always tried to balance life," Khaled continues, "sometimes it didn't work out, sometimes it was at the expense of the family, but I think all women make big sacrifices in their private lives, and they have to accept this. It's something that needs more study, to find ways to deal with this. When the boys were young they were always saying, 'why do you go to conferences? Why are you leaving us?' And during the First Intifada they were young and they used to miss me. But when they were older, I went on a political tour in Japan and I asked Bader if he wanted to come with me, and I told him that he had a duty to speak to young people and talk about the youth in Palestine. I wanted him to see the significance of what I was doing. Later Bashar went with me to South Africa, and when we came back he said, 'now I understand how important it is to speak to people.' He used to say, 'you go and speak to maybe a hundred or a thousand people, what about the millions watching TV? If you use arms again everybody will take notice of you, like in the old days, when you shoot everybody hears.'"

But, she admits, "I never thought before I had them that I would be so protective of my children." She has had to live throughout their childhood with the fear that they might be kidnapped or harmed because of her. Now, she has had to learn to let go. One of her sons has studied in London and neither, she says, has chosen to follow her and their father into political life. "But they were brought up in this way, with the ideas that we have but to have different opinions. The boys have their own ideas and we discuss them, at least to understand their ideas, but we agree on the main principles—that they are Palestinians, they have the right of return. And I deal with them on an equal basis and sometimes their friends tell them, we envy you for your parents because we see them speaking to you as if you are friends."

*　　*　　*

The move to Amman also had major implications for Khaled's political work. Since the events of Black September in 1970, Palestinian organizations have not been permitted in Jordan, and the PFLP, for obvious reasons, is deeply unpopular with the authorities. "They allow me to live here as a person and as a PNC member," says Khaled, "but I'm not allowed to speak as PFLP, even to the press. It's difficult, but I have to manage."

In the early 1990s Khaled found some organizations in Amman with which she could renew her political activities. Some were not specifically Palestinian but had been set up to support the Intifada in the West Bank and Gaza, others were established to collect donations for aid to Iraq. There was, she says, "this big front of women acting for Iraq, Palestine, and prisoners." But once political fervor stirred up by the US attack on Iraq diminished, "we were recognized and they began to restrict us," preventing organizations associated with the First Intifada or campaigning against the US sanctions on Iraq from functioning.

Khaled also describes how she was called to meet the Jordanian security services soon after the family moved there. "They told me, you are welcome here, but you know there are rules here. And I said, yes, I know." Testing the boundaries she would have to work within, Khaled accepted invitations to deliver lectures and give interviews and comments to the press.

Leila Khaled at home in Amman, September 2008 (Sarah Irving).

Leaving Damascus had also meant that Khaled had to leave her position in the leadership of the Syrian branch of the PFLP, but she remained on the party's Central Committee, to which she had been elected in 1981 and was re-elected in 1993 and 2000. In 1985 she left the leadership of the General Union of Palestinian Women after the PFLP temporarily withdrew its support from PLO organizations, but as of 2011 remains on its Administrative

Council. She is also still a PFLP representative on the Palestinian National Council, to which she was elected in 1979; and she continues to head the party's committee on Refugees and the Right of Return. These roles all mean constant travel, shuttling between Amman, Damascus, and other locations, something that as of 2011 she continues to do every few weeks.

*   *   *

The PFLP's relationship with the various organizations of the PLO and the Palestinian National Council has always been a tempestuous one. On several occasions during the 1970s the Popular Front withdrew its representatives on the PLO Executive Committee over the issue of negotiations with Israel, and it did so again in 1991. Problems increased after the Oslo Accords. But, stresses Leila Khaled, "still we are members of the PLO, we have our members on the executive committees, but we do not participate in the Palestinian Authority [PA]. The PNC and the Executive Committee represent all Palestinians, including Palestinians inside Palestine, but the PA is for Palestinians inside Palestine only and is a product of the Oslo process which we oppose. We were against establishing it, but we have to deal with it."

She also criticizes the Palestinian Authority—or Palestinian National Authority (PNA) as it is now known—for its policy of security cooperation with Israel under the Dayton Plan, which has led to US- and EU-trained Palestinian Authority forces arresting and in some cases killing members of Hamas. "[This] builds an apparatus not to defend our people, but to prevent our people from the resistance," claims Khaled. "Which means not only training, but also facing the resistance cells—all factions, not only Hamas. Meanwhile, every day Israel is entering any city, arresting people, assassinating them. Instead, the Palestinian Authority [should] strengthen those that are ready for resistance. Unfortunately this is one of the main contradictions ... the Palestinian Authority, whether in government, or the security apparatus or the police, are built in the Dayton vision, and not for the benefit of our people."[1] In 2011, Khaled added to her criticism of the PNA's program of security cooperation, pointing out that as well as Hamas, the Palestinian Authority had targeted members of Islamic Jihad and the PFLP. "For example, the PFLP's General Secretary Ahmed Sa'adat and four other PFLP members were arrested by the PA in 2002, and imprisoned in Jericho under the surveillance of US and British forces—an unprecedented situation," she said. "When the Israeli army attacked Jericho, they were moved to a prison in Israel, sentenced to long terms and are still being held in isolation."

The Palestinian Authority was established in 1994 under the Oslo Accords signed by the Fatah-dominated PLO and Israel. Seventeen years later, its status was still ambiguous. Large areas of the West Bank were still under Israeli military control (Areas B and C), while the towns and cities in Area A, though ostensibly under PNA jurisdiction, are ringed by Israeli settlements and checkpoints and subject to military incursions. The breakdown of relations between Fatah and Hamas after the latter's surprise victory in the 2006 elections had also split the areas under PNA control, with Fatah, the technical loser of the elections, maintaining its grip on the West Bank and a Hamas-led polity governing Gaza. As of summer 2011, a global campaign was underway to have the UN recognize Palestinian statehood—an effort that was almost certain to be blocked by Israel and the USA. The PFLP has maintained its rejection of the PA, arguing that it embodies the acceptance of a two-state solution, which the PFLP remains opposed to,[2] and that the current PNA structures are illegitimate unless new PNC elections are held.

The PFLP remains strongly opposed to the Oslo Accords with Israel, which do not implement the right of return for all Palestinian refugees. It also continues to reject the path of Fatah and the DFLP in accepting a two-state solution. In 2006, Khaled said of the outcomes of the 1990s Oslo peace process that "We witnessed how Arafat was pushed aside [and eventually besieged and killed, Khaled added in 2011], although he was the one who signed the Oslo Accords ... the US wanted to restore the face of Israel as a democracy and that Israel wanted peace. But what we have witnessed in the last ten years is how Israel has re-occupied the towns and cities and how they have pulled out of the accords."[3] The PFLP has, according to Khaled, called "for the rebuilding of the PLO and a renewed membership for the PNC, we are calling for elections for the PNC because this is our vision of how to rebuild the PLO and restore its position as a representative for all Palestinians everywhere."

It was her position on the PNC which in 1996 allowed Leila Khaled her one opportunity since her childhood to visit Palestine. The 1996 meeting of the Council was held in Gaza, part of an agreement between Yasser Arafat and Shimon Peres which saw amendments to the charter of the PLO. But the decision to go had not been an easy one. George Habash, then still General Secretary of the PFLP, declared that he would not enter Israeli borders until the right of return for refugees was implemented. "When the General Secretary declares a position it is difficult for others," says Khaled, "but in the Central Committee others were saying, 'well we used to go through the [Jordan] River and the Lebanese border to fight, and this is our country and it's good for any part of our people to go to our country.' So as the PFLP we were against it, but we are part of the PLO so we took the opportunity to go to Palestine, because we thought that if we didn't go at that time we might never have the chance."

Given her notoriety, it's hardly surprising that the idea of Leila Khaled being admitted into the West Bank and Gaza, and indeed crossing between them, attracted controversy in the Israeli and international press: "Three months before, calls from different parts of the world started, journalists coming to my house. Israelis started to call, one from *Yediot Ahronot*, one from television. When I heard them I just put down the phone, and they wrote that 'she won't speak to us.' The editor of the Middle East section of *Maariv*, he rang ten times and one of the ten times I answered and said, 'don't call me, when you leave our country I will talk to you,' and he wrote that." But the Israeli government insisted that Khaled's name was on a list of 154 people who had been "approved"—she wasn't even one of the 18 on whom more information was needed.[4]

Of course, despite the political process behind it and the inclusion of her name on the formal list of those to be admitted, the question of whether Leila Khaled would actually be able to pass through Israeli border controls was an open one, right up to the last minute.

A few days before she was due to travel, says Khaled, an Israeli military spokesperson had announced that she would not be admitted unless she signed a document condemning terrorism and backing the peace process. When she first reached the border crossing at King Hussein Bridge, which crosses the Jordan River and enters the West Bank near Jericho, she refused to sign the Israeli paper, and was duly turned back. "I'm not going to sign any document," she told them. "This is not a peace process, it's just a process." But having prepared psychologically for months to visit Palestine Khaled was, she admits, "very upset."

But the Israeli refusal to admit Khaled wasn't just a personal challenge to her, but a contradiction of the agreement between Yasser Arafat and Shimon Peres, and as such it had wider repercussions. According to Khaled, "Arafat told the Israelis, you are turning back PNC members and we agreed that PNC members and their families could enter. If you turn her back it means you may turn others back, and that violates our agreement." So Khaled returned to King Hussein Bridge, "and I waited and waited, and I was called by the Shin Bet [Israeli intelligence]," she describes: "There was a very small room with two men sitting behind the counter, one holding a computer, and the other, a very ugly man with very little eyes, looking at me, and a women from the army."

More than a quarter of a century on, Khaled persisted in the kind of defiant games that had so frustrated David Frew in Ealing police station. On being asked her name she insisted that since they had invited her to their office, they must know it. She refused to answer the Shin Bet's questions, and when challenged by one of the officers with being "against peace," she responded "which peace? When I don't see you there is peace, when I come to my country without being interrogated, you don't have the right to interrogate me."

"He didn't answer this," continues Khaled. "He just said, so you are with terrorism! I said to him, I am the first one who held arms against you? Occupation is terrorism. He didn't respond.

I wanted to provoke him, you know, when we provoke people who are interrogating they get nervous.

The other one, I felt he wanted to kill me. He started to ask questions. He asked me, 'do you intend to try to delete the items in the constitution that call for the destruction of Israel?' In the constitution it's not like that, because the PLO was established in 1964, so in the constitution it's to liberate Palestine, the West Bank, and Gaza were not occupied, and the constitution is for Palestinians outside and inside, like that, there is no item saying 'destruction of Israel.' I answered him, 'this is none of your business, it is our business.' And he said 'OK, do you have relatives in Israel.' And I said, 'you are speaking about the 1948 area, of course,' and he said 'can you name them?' And I said 'can I name 850,000 people?' And he said, 'but there are 950,000.' I said 'yes, but 100,000 are your agents, and they are not related to me.' But he mentioned one of my cousins, he said 'what about Samir?' And I said, 'I told you, they are all my relatives, they are all my people, all my family, and you go and get your answer from the government not from me.' But sometimes he was just haggling, asking 'what is the best thing you have done in your life?' I said, 'what are you, are you a journalist? I will tell you, the best thing I have done in my life is I took up arms against you.' The other man was laughing, and saying, 'what are you going to do with the arms now?' And I said, 'I'm not going to tell you what I would do with the arms.'"

Despite the mutual hostility and suspicion, Khaled's confrontation with the Shin Bet only lasted a quarter of an hour. Other PNC members were interrogated for many hours or held overnight. "They meant first of all to humiliate us and secondly to know who all these PNC members are," claims Khaled. Other council members, she says, later told her that they were sure the Israeli security "simply wanted to study us."

But even getting past the Israeli intelligence wasn't the end of the tortuous process of entering Palestine. Passing through the border crossing, "a woman police officer came to me and shouted, 'don't you believe in peace, Leila?' And I turned my head away. And she came again and said, 'don't you believe in peace?' And I said, 'when I don't see you here, I will say peace is in this territory.'"

The disruption continued outside. A group of Israeli settlers with placards reading "Peres, Leila Tov" (a message to Israeli leader Shimon Peres, perceived by right-wing settler groups as a "dove," and a play on Khaled's name and on the Hebrew for "good night") were scattered when a Palestinian security officer shot in the air, panicking the Israeli soldiers in the border control building. As she was about to leave the building, a Palestinian official approached Khaled, telling her to jump in his car as she exited, because there were suspicions that the Israeli security services might try to force her into a military vehicle and take her away. She was whisked away, and finally had the chance to see Palestine—the West Bank and Gaza—for the first time in decades.

"Sometimes they are fiery, but sometimes they are OK," says Khaled of Palestinian National Council meetings. They include plenaries where senior members—sometimes the chairmen or general secretaries—of the various factions lay out their positions on the various issues on the agenda. Committees on various national problems split off and discuss resolutions and bring them back to further plenary gatherings and votes are taken. Historically the proceedings have often been dominated by the big names of the Palestinian resistance movement, and Khaled's comments on the many PNC sessions she has attended are peppered with phrases like "Arafat refused." And, she admits, many of the most important discussions and decisions happen outside the official meetings, in corridors and kitchens, "and not everyone always follows what his party says." But, she says, PNC sessions are also an important meeting point for people from all across the Palestinian political spectrum. "We come from all over the world, we have members of the PNC living in the United States, Europe, Latin America, and in Arab countries, so it's a unique experience when they come together every four years." The meeting in Gaza, for the many PNC members who had been denied access to their homeland for decades, was a deeply emotional event.

Eyewitness accounts of other PNC sessions tell similar stories. In 1987 the PNC's eighteenth session took place in Algiers and was described in one British newspaper as "an event that is a slightly bizarre cross between a party conference, a class reunion and a huge emotional wedding." Leila was at that PNC session too; by this time, press descriptions of her noted that she looked "dumpier and more matronly" than in her hijacking days. The appearance of her male colleagues on the Council was not commented on.[5]

As the Gaza Congress drew to a close, the PFLP members hoped to stay longer in Gaza, but at midnight they were called by Palestinian security and told that Israeli orders were for all of them to leave immediately. "We refused to go," says Khaled. "The men went, but the women refused, because if we left then we cannot go back." But the PNC members were all too aware of the restrictions they might face if they continued to defy the order to leave. "We had heard the stories from Erez [the border crossing from the north of Gaza into Israel], the families, the men, women and children waiting there, who could not go back into Gaza and were not allowed out. There was a Palestinian family living in Canada who came to Gaza through Cairo and they thought they could go out through Erez, so they went inside the border crossing where you can't go out except through the other side and they were there for a week. So I was waiting to see if my husband and children got permission to come but they were refused, so I had to leave, and I came back here to Amman."

*   *   *

Since the beginning of the First Intifada, the PFLP has had to negotiate new political relationships, dealing not only with its old comrades and adversaries in Fatah but also with the rising Islamist movements, particularly Hamas. On the core issue for most of the parties, that of Palestine's standing vis-à-vis Israel and the status of the various peace negotiations, the PFLP has found common ground with Hamas in opposing the Oslo Accords. Recognizing its current political weakness, the PFLP has at times tried to broker peace between Fatah and Hamas, whose conflict has resulted in killings and episodes of torture and imprisonment on both sides, in both the Fatah-controlled West Bank and in Gaza under Hamas. "It's a terrible thing, it's terrible for us," says Khaled, "we're trying our best as part of the Palestinian movement to bring them together to negotiate because the division is very destructive on our people, especially those living in Gaza." In late 2009, she added: "[The PFLP] and others are calling for reconciliation between these two factions because it is not in the interests of our people. It has weakened the Palestinians (vis-à-vis) Israel, and also weakened solidarity with Palestinian human rights on the international level ... We don't think Hamas has used its legitimacy in the right way. They got a majority in the elections,' but they shouldn't have gone to the extent of solving the contradictions between them and Fatah with the use of arms."[6] Speaking in 2011, Khaled extended this critique to Fatah as well as Hamas.

As of August 2011, the "March 15 Movement" demonstrations which took place in the West Bank and Gaza, calling for national unity and an end to the Fatah–Hamas conflict, had succeeded in bringing about a hypothetical deal, but this was stalled by PNA President Mahmoud Abbas' insistence on retaining the increasingly unpopular neoliberal Salam Fayyad as his prime minister.[7] In November 2011, Khaled said again that "we are still pressing to end the split and promote a meeting between Meshal and Abu Mazen and for national dialogue with all the factions. We must end the division because it is destroying our struggle."

But despite their common position on negotiation with Israel, Khaled is still skeptical about Hamas as a movement. "Before it declared itself as Hamas," she emphasizes, "they were the Muslim Brotherhood and they were against us, and they were all the time talking against the Left." The growth of the Islamist movements in contrast to the decline of the PFLP and other left-wing parties has, Khaled believes, a range of causes. Disillusionment with the failure of the Oslo process and the corruption of the Palestinian Authority have, she believes, driven people to seek new representatives. And, she points out, during the First Intifada and Oslo periods the Israeli security agencies and their international supporters were still more concerned about the left, with its history of armed struggle, than with religious movements they perceived as more benign. "In the 1990s," says Khaled, "some of our cadres left the PFLP and around 500 of its main activists were in jail and there was the assassination of our General Secretary Abu Ali Mustafa. So people felt that neither the right-wing represented by Fatah could solve any problems and it was corrupt, and the left cannot be a substitute for it, so where is the new force for change? Islam is our culture, and Hamas worked socially before they showed themselves, and this is very intelligent. They established universities, schools, hospitals, health centers, and supported poor people, so when they declared themselves they were accepted. And then they went on suicide operations in Israel and people felt that this is the way, because this way we are still resisting."

In the tradition of left-wing self-criticism, Khaled partly blames her own movement for its failure to work hard enough to convince people with its programs. But she also situates it in the context of wider geopolitical developments—the decline of the Soviet bloc and therefore of the military and financial resources available to left-wing organizations, and the rise of political Islam across the Middle East, with Iran as a lesson that it is possible to expel US-backed regimes. Khaled's PFLP Political Bureau colleague Khalida Jarrar has elaborated on this issue, saying that

> no leftist political party can do a lot by itself. Now the leftists are facing a difficult situation: we have no power, no money, no international support. Even in the Arab world, the Islamic groups are now getting the lion's share. We are facing internal problems, like the economic one. We are poor parties, and if you want to raise social programs, you need money to do it. How can we compete against Hamas that has a lot of infrastructure and funds? People do not want just talks, but actions on the social level.[8]

But, Khaled suggests, the Islamist organizations may face a similar fate to that of the PFLP and Fatah. The internecine killings in Gaza will, Khaled thinks, show people that Hamas "are all the same" and as corrupt as Fatah, while the many assassinations carried out against Hamas and Islamic Jihad leaders may weaken the movements in the same way as the killing of Abu Ali Mustafa and imprisonment of Ahmed Sa'adat did for the PFLP. "They don't want to have more prisoners, they just want to kill the activists" says Khaled of the Israeli authorities.

On practices such as suicide bombing, with which Hamas is strongly associated in the West, Khaled remains ambivalent, but certainly does not issue a complete rejection. "We told the Hamas leaders, it's a tactic, not a strategic line in the struggle, because it's a culture and an education of death. It's about death, not about life," she declares. Perhaps ironically given her own role in the attachment of the label "hijacker" to the Palestinian people, she also criticizes the practice for "turning the world against us, to all the world we are just terrorists now." The PFLP's Abu Ali Mustafa Brigades—named for the party's general secretary, assassinated by Israel—claimed responsibility for several suicide bombings in 2002 and 2003, including that of a market in Netanya in May 2002 and two in the West Bank settlements of Karnei Shomron and Ariel in February and March 2002 respectively.[9] Khaled justifies these as a very specific military tactic used in the face of the massive Operation Defensive Shield re-occupation of the West Bank and Gaza by the Israeli army and air force in 2002. "Sometimes we use this tactic, like when they attacked in 2002. If a few people do it, it can be justified, but not all the time," she says.

Khaled also objects to suicide bombing because she believes that, to young Palestinians, it dehumanizes the idea of struggle: "We don't want this generation to think they can just fight by pushing the button. It's not on the internet, it's their lives. So we don't justify it, but we cannot condemn it. These are our people also, those young people are our people, we can't condemn someone who is dead, who sacrificed their lives. We told them [Hamas] that we don't see this as the best way to mobilize the people."

In an interview in 2010, Khaled expanded on this position, noting the desperation that has driven young people "who also dream of a good future and a bright future [to] go and explode themselves," saying that "Israel minimizes the distance between life and death to the extent that they [suicide bombers] didn't see a difference between death and life." She also claims that interventions by the left-wing factions have helped to cut the numbers of suicide bombings committed by the Islamist groups. "We have advised our brothers in Hamas and Al Jihad that using this, it's a controversial thing so they have stopped it ... now it has stopped and I think they realized that such action is not for the interests of the struggle."[10]

But, like many Palestinians and supporters of a just peace in the Middle East, Khaled also justifiably objects to the West's obsession with suicide bombers. Due to the high media profile given to Israeli civilians killed by Palestinians, and particularly to suicide bombing, analyses of Western media coverage such as the samples and focus groups described by Greg Philo and Mike Berry in 2004 demonstrate how skewed Western perceptions of the situation are. A majority of Philo and Berry's audience samples thought that more Israelis than Palestinians were killed in the conflict, or that casualty numbers were about the same, and analysis of news coverage emphasized that Palestinians were often described more actively as attackers and killers (Israeli military actions, by contrast, just resulted in Palestinians "being killed"). Israeli dead were given much more airtime and were more "personalized," with case studies and stories which elevated them above the status of mere casualty numbers.[11] Statistics collated by Israeli human rights organization B'Tselem paint a very different picture to that painted in the Western press, showing that between the beginning of the Second Intifada in 2000 and the end of 2008 (i.e. not taking into account the bulk of the deaths from the Operation Cast Lead invasion of December 2008–January 2009), Palestinian casualties in the Occupied Territories numbered over 4,800 while Israeli casualties were around 480. Despite frequent emphasis by Israel and its supporters on its assassination of "militants" or "terrorists" amongst these figures, the number of Palestinian minors killed in the same period was 952, against 39 Israelis.[12]

In contrast to some Palestinian commentators (and indeed attempted suicide bombers themselves), Khaled does not see the fact that young women have undertaken such operations as showing that women have advanced in Palestinian society.[13]

Although throughout her own life she has sought to prove that women can fight just as ably as men, and she still adheres completely to the necessity for armed struggle against the Occupation, she told an interviewer in 2002 that "We in the PFLP have always considered men and women as equal. My comrades accepted me from the beginning and called on me to do the military actions years ago. There was no difference and I never felt as if I didn't have their respect. Today there is an increasing religious influence in our society. When the religious leaders say that women who undertake suicide operations are finally equal to men, I have a problem. Everyone is equal in death—rich, poor, Arab, Jew, Christian, we are all equal. I would rather see women equal to men in life."[14]

In keeping with this view, Leila Khaled has also expressed her concerns about the impact that the rise of the Islamist parties has had on the position of women in the West Bank and Gaza. Many Palestinian feminists have since the early 1990s voiced anxiety about a backlash against the partial progress which Palestinian women made in the 1970s and '80s, in both personal independence and institutional rights. The failure of the mainstream parties to stand up for women's rights during conflict over the "violent imposition of the headscarf" in Gaza in the late 1980s sent a signal to women activists that the male leaderships of the factions would sacrifice their rights if it was necessary to maintain their other political alliances.[15] In a series of incidents in spring and summer 1988, graffiti calling on women to dress "modestly" and to wear the hijab as a mark of respect for the martyrs of the Intifada appeared in Gaza. Isolated activists, including Aitemad Muhanna of the PFLP-affiliated Palestinian Women's Committees, stood up to these demands, reportedly saying that "I shall not wear it even if I become the martyr of the veil." However, the leadership of both the left-wing parties and of the party-affiliated women's organizations failed to back their grassroots members. Some, such as Eileen Kuttab of the PWC's development wing, did feel that enforcement of the veil could see women driven from public life, but other members of the leadership were more worried that a confrontation with Hamas would result in a dangerous split in Palestinian society, at the height of the First Intifada.[16] Muhanna herself, in a conference presentation at SOAS in London in spring 2010, said of the left-wing parties that they "mostly failed to internalize their ideology among the population, because they maintained an artificial divorce between national politics and ideology on the one hand, and popular social and cultural change on the other. They feared to antagonize popular opinion by openly mobilizing against traditional systems of values, especially those based on patriarchy and/or Islam."[17] Speaking from Gaza to a Russian newspaper, Mariam Abu Dagga, Leila Khaled's colleague on the PFLP Political Bureau, says that at the age of 58 it is still an issue that she refuses to wear the headscarf:

> here I am ... the only woman without a headscarf, the only woman smoking. A Brother asked me to cover my head with the red flag of the Popular Front. And I said that I had left the house as one of Abu Dagga, and I came back as a faithful daughter of Palestine. I gave all my life to Palestine. If I had put the headscarf on, mullahs would have been proud of me, but that way they were shy in my presence ... Now when a woman acts bravely and on her own, everybody understands that she is from the Popular Front. And I am their example and protector.[18]

Although the Gaza incident is fairly well-known, similar events also took place in the West Bank, in the city of Hebron. There, however, the men who were harassing unveiled women in the street were seized by PFLP activists and found to be not Hamas members, but known local collaborators with the Israeli intelligence.[19] In the senior ranks of Hamas itself, the only ministerial portfolio held by a woman has been that of Minister for Women's Affairs, Myriam Saleh. According to Khaled Hroub, Hamas has many female activists, especially in universities and amongst graduates, but its women's committees are primarily concerned—like the Palestinian women's movement prior to the 1970s—with "traditional spheres" such as charities and schools. Large-scale mobilization of women activists is, says Hroub, vitally important to Hamas' electoral successes, but "At other levels, mainly leadership, in Hamas women disappear ... Compared with the broader Palestinian national movement,

where many female figures have left a political impact at the
public and leadership level, Hamas's women are almost invisible
to the outside world."[20]

As Leila Khaled puts it, "I think that they [Hamas and Jihad]
have a different vision. When we discussed this with them, they
said 'we believe in equity but not in equality.' Although people
say that Islam gave women their rights, in implementation
it's not equal. In the internal rules of Hamas, the mission of
a woman is to be educated so she can bring up an educated
generation. In the elections they nominated seven women but
this is because the election law in Palestine says that the third
name on each list should be a woman. They have their beliefs
about the role of women, but they don't believe that women
can be part of the decision makers. Even Fatah has women in
the Central Committee, but we don't see women in Hamas or
Jihad. Women, when they bear arms, are participating in the
national struggle. That's why in the Palestinian Declaration of
Independence in 1988 there is a paragraph about women, that
in a liberated, independent state, women are equal with men in
rights and duties."

7
Leila Khaled's Future, Palestine's Future

"Retire? From what? I will only retire when I go back to Haifa," laughed Leila Khaled in 2008. In 2000, with its cadres ageing, the PFLP allocated retirement ages of 55 for women and 65 for men. Nearly ten years beyond the age at which she could retire, Khaled insists that "You can't retire from struggle, or from being involved. I may not take the same positions, because a human being can give all they have, physically, from maybe 20, 25 until 45, all their capacity, with enthusiasm. Physically, it's something scientific that half of a human being's life he goes up and then he comes down, but also the will is important. Everything that has happened, of course it affected me psychologically speaking, but still I have the will."

"So," she continues, "I don't think I will [retire]. I thought about it, that the situation is getting harder, but it doesn't mean that when it gets harder I retire. Of course it depends on the conference, if they want to elect me or not, that's something that's not in my hands. Until now, I'll go on. I don't know after 10 years if I will still be alive." The husky laugh with which Khaled delivers these thoughts has a lot to do with the cigarette which she permanently holds in one hand. "She's so committed and at her age she could take the soft option and settle for family life," says Linda Clair, a friend of Khaled's since the 1980s. "I can't imagine anything stopping her, but I just wish she'd give up smoking. She needs a funnel on her head." In a follow-up interview, conducted in 2011, the cigarette is still visible on the Skype screen as Khaled gesticulates.

But neither her mid sixties nor her nicotine addiction seem to be slowing Leila Khaled down. As well as her regular trips between Amman and Damascus to fulfill her PFLP roles, she has refused the ideological and organizational fossilization which beset many left-wing organizations and activists after the fall of the Soviet Union. She has embraced the role of civil society—both Palestinian and international—as a force alongside her party's more conventional belief in armed struggle and party politics.

Khaled credits international activist groups such as the International Solidarity Movement with raising awareness of the realities of the Israeli Occupation throughout the world. "When Rachel Corrie was killed, it raised the consciousness of our young people that an American student came and defended houses like this," she says. "When they see groups from abroad coming just to see and to support the Palestinians, it means we are not alone and it educates our people. In the past we had foreign visitors and we discovered that the Israelis had sent them as spies, so it took time for our people to trust foreigners who came to support us. But international solidarity is one of the elements that will give hope to our people that on the level of civil society, popular pressure will make governments change their attitude."

Khaled has also continued to appear at international conferences. Once these were mainly UN and Soviet-sponsored gatherings of women's rights campaigners or socialist activists, but now she is a regular sight at World Social Forums, major civil society conferences which have grown out of the first WSF, held at Porto Alegre in Brazil in 2001. Khaled herself has said that they are "very important. It's a time when people can meet from different parts of the world, we can network with other movements, and build solidarity."[1] She has spoken at World Social Forums in India, Brazil, and Kenya, participating in workshops on issues ranging from American policy in the Middle East to children's rights and, of course, the situation for Palestinians in the West Bank, Gaza, and diaspora. Her presence at WSFs has not been without controversy; in Kenya in 2007 she became embroiled in arguments over the wording of conference declarations which equated support for the Palestinian struggle with support for Israeli anti-occupation groups, even if these groups didn't agree with the Palestinians' right of return or the sharing of Jerusalem. In her view, the latter should have been covered in a separate paragraph.

Leila Khaled with Brazilian radical cartoonist Carlos Latuff at the World Social Forum in Nairobi, 2007 (Carlos Latuff).

Having learnt from experiences such as her encounter with Felicia Langer in the early 1980s, Khaled doesn't dismiss the possibility of working with some Israelis and praises Israeli activists such as those who join weekly demonstrations against the Separation Wall at the West Bank village of Bil'in. But on the subject of working with the wider Israeli peace movement, she maintains a harder line: "The problem is if you deal with people who are not supporting your struggle and who are not really against the occupation, this is a waste of time and it creates an illusion, because if you see people working together, organizing activities together, they think that's peace, but in reality it's not peace. We discovered that most of these groups, whether they call themselves Peace Now or refuseniks, stop if you talk about two issues. They don't talk about Jerusalem. And with the refugees, they say these are living in other Arab countries, why do they want this land? So temporarily we could benefit from working with them, but this is not a strategic thing unless they change their minds. There is a difference between supporting the Palestinian people's rights and supporting them on humanitarian issues."

At other Forums conflict has broken out over the issue of calls for sanctions against Israel. Some of these have not necessarily been disagreements about the legitimacy of sanctions calls, but about the impacts of tactics such as sanctions on governments or their populations and who constitutes the legitimate targets of boycotts. With Leila Khaled and her PFLP comrades still very much in a mindset that sees power and responsibility as lying with states and governments, it is unsurprising that she has at times clashed with activists who espouse less state-based strategies and aspirations, although Khaled has called for "a similar campaign to that that was run against the South African Government during the Apartheid regime."[2] She describes how "we stayed for two days discussing this, and people came from different groups and in the end they accepted sanctions. I said, you participated in your forum and I'm just saying that even in such forums you have differences, people maybe change their ideas or are pressurized. But the main thing is that a better world is possible and under it the movement against globalization and imperialism and so on. I said the first thing is that we are all against occupation. Change needs to be in the countries and governments, but it is also important to change minds, so that they support you with your vision, not only with others' vision."

In common with the organizational discipline of the PFLP, however, Khaled still seems uncomfortable at times with the focus on her as an individual. "I was invited to a WSF in Sri Lanka, and I couldn't go," she says. "I apologized and said I could send somebody else, but they didn't accept that. People think they want *this* person. I told them, I am part of a party, not just for myself, so we can send someone else, but they didn't allow it. Maybe individuals still have an impact."

As well as the activist gatherings of the WSF, Khaled's high profile has turned her into a kind of ambassador for the PFLP and a wider Palestinian constituency, visiting the likes of controversial

Nicaraguan president Daniel Ortega in November 2010,[3] and speaking at an election rally for the Labour, Democracy and Freedom bloc in the southern Turkish city of Mersin in June 2011.[4] Arriving in Sweden to give a seminar and speak at a rally in Stockholm, opponents reported her to the police, but no action was taken;[5] and it was Khaled's well-known name which appeared on the PFLP's statement of solidarity to striking Italian metalworkers in February 2011, with the words: "It's time to change, it's time to revolt against all kinds of oppression and corruption. It's time to establish a new system based on social justice, freedom of speech and expression."[6] Most recently, she appeared as a witness at the South African hearings of the Russell Tribunal on Palestine.

With the "Arab Revolution" uprisings across the Middle East and North Africa in late 2010 and 2011 there has been a resurgence of interest in broadly left-wing ideas and social change across the region. Western assumptions that unrest and regime change would lead to a wave of Islamic governments were challenged by the huge demonstrations which, far from calling for Sharia law or a global Caliphate, demanded an end to (often Western-backed) authoritarian regimes and neoliberal economic policies.[7]

Despite the revelations in the "Palestine Papers" in January 2011, including the fact that senior Fatah negotiators had offered Israel concessions well beyond those backed by the majority of Palestinian society,[8] the Arab Spring has not brought about the mass protests against the PNA which some commentators hoped for at the start of 2011. But Palestinians did mobilize to call for an end to strife between the Fatah and Hamas factions, and the Arab Spring has emboldened anti-settlement and Apartheid Wall protesters in the West Bank, giving them a wider context in which to frame their struggle. "We feel that now we have a back[ing]," a female protester at An-Nabi Saleh was quoted as saying in a MERIP report.[9] While acknowledging that the Palestinian March 15 youth movement, which in 2011 called for unity between Fatah and Hamas, does not have an alternative strategy, Khaled believes that Palestinians draw strength from the Arab awakening.

Leila Khaled's name has not been totally absent from the March 15 movement's discourse. Palestinian-American journalist Ahmed Moor, writing in the East Jerusalem-based *This Week in Palestine*, cited her staunch rejection of the Oslo Accords and the PNA, saying that "In the aftermath of the Palestine Papers, young Palestinians can look to her legacy for a model of legitimate and dignified struggle in the face of adversity. Her revolutionary past and her present-day insistence on Palestinian rights continue to inspire young activists in both Palestine and the diaspora."[10]

According to Khaled herself, "the results of the revolutions in Tunisia and Egypt are still unseen," she believes. "In the Tunisian case, the Islamists have won. It's because the leftists are not united and the Islamists are the most organized. After the revolutions the US administration wanted to confine the results, so they accepted the falls of Ben Ali and Mubarak. But Egypt is always the milestone of change in the Arab World—it was under Nasser and it is again. I know elections are the democratic way, but it's a matter of who the USA and the West in general are supporting with their money. I think they will try to strengthen the moderate Islamist movements and try to divert hostility in the Arab World away from Israel and towards Iran."

Khaled has also publicly linked the regional and international Palestine liberation movements with the various struggles for social and human rights across the Arab world and beyond.[11] Her position, she says, reflects the PFLP's long-standing strategy linking the Palestinian struggle with a broader Arab national democratic revolution. "This is a global class struggle," she said in November 2011. "The poor are filling the streets in two continents—North America and Europe—and even in Israel calling for social justice. The Israeli government is trying to bribe the young people to move into the settlements, but they refuse, deciding for themselves. Israel is facing problems—that's why they are always raiding Gaza, because when they raid Gaza people support the government. When the Israelis have a crisis they solve it by external war. And now the crisis of the capitalist system is emerging, so we see people rallying in Wall Street and across Europe. Merkel and Sarkozy are occupying Greece, and

China is doing its job by invading the world with their products. They are brilliant enough to launch products not wars. But the rich are only a small class on the global level."

*   *   *

Khaled says that over the last ten years the requests for newspaper, radio, and TV interviews which she has always received have increased. She seems almost gleeful at the challenges some journalists have faced, and the insights they have involuntarily been given into the daily lives of most Palestinians:

"One French woman called me and said, I want to make a film about you. I said OK, just tell me what you want to do, and she wanted to film in Haifa. I said I couldn't go there and she asked, why not? I told her, you go to the Israeli embassy and ask. She got a visa to make a film in Haifa, but she didn't tell them what film. Then she asked for a visa for me, and they took her visa away from her. She called me and said, those bastards! I said OK, now I'll tell you the story, and she got very upset; she had read all these things but she never imagined it would be like this for her."

According to Khaled, Lina Makboul, who made the prizewinning documentary film *Leila Khaled: Hijacker*, faced similar challenges. She encountered the customary searches and interrogations when she visited Israel to interview the pilot of one of the planes Khaled hijacked. But, says Khaled, Makboul also had her budget stopped and new conditions put on the production by the Swedish TV station she worked for. Only the documentary's enthusiastic reception at film festivals around Europe finally got it shown on the television station it had been intended for.

Not surprisingly, Leila Khaled is also often asked if she plans to write her memoirs. She tried to allocate some time to do so in 1996 but, she says, "I found that at that time it was a struggle for me, it was busy and there were so many pulls from outside, and for writing you need to be stable. It's easy for me to speak but not to write." Her husband Fayez has suggested that she works with someone else, employed to transcribe her words; another friend said that she should do the job by herself to maintain the passion with which she speaks.

Khaled puts the idea of her own words or her own autobiography firmly in the context of the history of her movement. She compares herself to oral history projects working in Ramallah and Gaza to record the experiences of women prisoners. And she recalls earlier efforts to document the history of the Palestinian resistance—which perhaps serve as an incentive not to set down the facts of her own life. "We had a big center in Beirut in the 1970s," she says. "It was a Palestine

Leila Khaled continues to intrigue and inspire young Palestinians, Palestine solidarity activists, and political radicals around the world. This image is from *The Hookah Girl*, a zine in which artist Marguerite Dabaie explores her own experiences of growing up Palestinian-Christian in the USA (www.margoyle.net) (Marguerite Dabaie).

Research Center. When the Israelis came it was the first place they went to and they took everything. Only after the PLO went to court did they return some of the research. When they were asked why they were taking it all, one of the leaders said: because we want to know what you think about us."

Leila Khaled has countless stories of people from all over the world—from Pakistan, the UK, Jordan, and Lebanon—who have called their children after her. She has a letter from a Japanese woman telling her that she wanted to name her daughter Leila, but that because the letter L doesn't really work in Japanese, she couldn't, but made up her own equivalent. Despite the accusations of arrogance made against her by the likes of Robin Morgan,[12] Khaled seems genuinely humbled by this. "This was very touching to me," she says of a man who brought his young daughter, Leila, to visit her in her hotel in Pakistan at 5 a.m., having travelled hundreds of miles. "Whenever people tell me that, I feel honored by it while at the same time I feel a responsibility. I feel it, and it gives me strength. When the situation is hard, it gives me the strength to go on with the same will. Because these are my people, those young ones are named after me, it means I should go on. I've forgotten many things in this life but this I remember, that this is a responsibility, that these people gave my name, and I really am proud of it."

Leila Khaled has been part of the struggle for a homeland for the Palestinian people for half a century. She has seen peace processes come and go, superpowers and regional players shift their allegiances and tactics, leaderships take one position and another. There is a certain weariness in her contribution to the "When I Return" project, which has collected the individual dreams of Palestinians reflecting on their first act if they could return to their homeland. "When I return to Palestine, I will sleep under an orange tree for three days," was Khaled's line.[13]

"It's always the future of the people," she says. "I don't even discuss it, I just believe in it. It's a reality for me. We learned from history that there is not always occupation and resistance, it's not the fundamental equation. But where there is occupation, there will always be resistance. In the history of Palestine, the Romans, the Crusaders, and the Ottomans came, but the Palestinians stayed there. Wherever there is occupation we have hard work to do, but always we have the will, generation after generation. I believe in my people and I believe that we have people all around the world supporting our struggle"

"At the beginning," she continues, "we said that we will never co-exist with the Israelis. But I tell you, if there are 4 or 5 million and we want to get them out—it's not logical. Those children who were born there, it's not their fault that their parents came and settled down. But that means that the key to this conflict is the right of return for refugees. This may take another 50 years. I say a homeland is worth all we have to implement, to achieve the goals of our struggle. We look at Israeli society—there are different voices from those of the past, there are voices against occupation, against the apartheid system, against the policies of the government, those who refuse the army, many voices saying why are we always going to war? And women with their pictures of their sons and daughters who were killed, these people will not wait for life, they will do something. This doesn't depend upon our plans. But unless the core issues, the land and the refugees, are dealt with in a just way this conflict will go from one generation to another. All these elements of the struggle and the conflict will gather together. It will work itself out."

"I don't think it will be in my lifetime, but for other generations."

Notes

INTRODUCTION

1. Rosemary Sayigh, *Palestinians: From Peasants to Revolutionaries* (London: Zed Books, 1979), 144–52.
2. Robin Morgan, *The Demon Lover: On the Sexuality of Terrorism* (London: Mandarin 1989), 252.
3. See, for example, http://saroujah.blogspot.com/2005/03/life-on-death-row.html and http://robertlindsay.blogspot.com/2006/03/pflp-leader-saadat-seized-in-jericho.html
4. Fawzia Afzal-Khan, "Bridging the Gap Between So-Called Postcolonial and Minority Women of Color: A Comparative Methodology for Third World Feminist Literary Criticism," in *Womanist Theory and Research*, vols. 2.1–2.2 (1996–97).
5. Quoted in Miriam Shaviv, "Fighting For Their Own Liberation," *Jerusalem Post*, February 8, 2002.
6. Morgan, *The Demon Lover*, 211.
7. Ibid.

CHAPTER 1

1. Mary Eliza Rogers, *Domestic Life in Palestine* (London: Kegan Paul 1862/1989), 85.
2. Martin Gilbert, *Israel: A History* (London: Doubleday 1998), 22, 50, 54.
3. Ibid., 61.
4. Ibid., 94.
5. Albert Hourani, *A History of the Arab Peoples* (London: Faber & Faber, 1991), 321–2.
6. Ibid., 324, 384, and Benny Morris (ed.), *Making Israel* (Ann Arbor: University of Michigan Press, 2007), 21.
7. Gilbert, *Israel: A History*, 132.
8. Ibid., 158, 162.
9. Morris, *Making Israel*, 21.
10. Ibid., 20.
11. Gilbert, *Israel: A History*, 162.
12. Morris, *Making Israel*, 22.
13. Leila Khaled and George Hajjar, *My People Shall Live: The Autobiography of a Revolutionary* (London: Hodder & Stoughton, 1973), 24.

14. Daniel McGowan and Marc H. Ellis, *Remembering Deir Yassin: The Future of Israel and Palestine* (New York: Olive Branch Press, 1998), 3.

15. Khaled, *My People Shall Live*, 25.

16. Ibid., 26.

17. Ibid., 28.

18. Eileen MacDonald, *Shoot the Women First* (London: Arrow Books, 1991), 97.

19. Ibid., 30–1.

20. Ibid., 43.

21. Ibid., 44–5.

22. May 15 was the date of the British withdrawal of its Mandate from Palestine, opening the way for the declaration of the State of Israel.

23. The 1917 Balfour Declaration was a letter from the British Foreign Secretary to Lord Rothschild, stating that "His Majesty's government view with favour the establishment in Palestine of a national home for the Jewish people, and will use their best endeavours to facilitate the achievement of this object, it being clearly understood that nothing shall be done which may prejudice the civil and religious rights of existing non-Jewish communities in Palestine, or the rights and political status enjoyed by Jews in any other country."

24. Khaled, *My People Shall Live*, 44.

25. R. K. Karanjia, *Arab Dawn* (London: Lawrence & Wishart 1959), 172–4.

26. Robert Fisk, *Pity the Nation: Lebanon at War* (Oxford: Oxford University Press, 1990/2001), 69–73.

27. Walid Kazziha, *Revolutionary Transformation in the Arab World: Habash and his Comrades from Nationalism to Marxism* (London/Tonbridge: Charles Knight & Co, 1975), 32, 63–4.

28. Khaled, *My People Shall Live*, 45.

29. Ibid., 48.

30. MacDonald, *Shoot the Women First*, 105.

31. Khaled, *My People Shall Live*, 47.

32. Kazziha, *Revolutionary Transformation in the Arab World*, 20–1.

33. MacDonald, *Shoot the Women First*, 105.

34. Khaled, *My People Shall Live*, 38–9.

35. MacDonald, *Shoot the Women First*, 104.

36. Khaled, *My People Shall Live*, 51.

37. Ibid., 53.

38. As'ad AbuKhalil, "Internal Contradictions in the PFLP: Decision Making and Policy Determination," *Middle East Journal*, vol. 41. no. 3 (Summer, 1987), 364–5.

39. Khaled, *My People Shall Live*, 59.

40. Ibid., 63.

41. Ibid., 76.

42. Ibid., 79.

43. Ibid., 84.

44. Ibid., 80.
45. Muhsin Ibrahim in *Al-Hurriya*, May 2, 1960, quoted in Kazziha, *Revolutionary Transformation in the Arab World*, 65.
46. Kazziha, *Revolutionary Transformation*, 67–80; George Habache and Georges Malbrunot, *Les revolutionnaires ne meurent jamais: conversations avec Georges Malbrunot* (Paris: Editions Fayard, 2008), Chapters 3–5.
47. Alain Gresh, *The PLO: The Struggle Within* (London: Zed Books, 1983), 26.
48. Khaled, *My People Shall Live*, 90.
49. Kazziha, *Revolutionary Transformation in the Arab World*, 83–4.
50. Raid El-Rayyes and Dunia Nahas, *Guerrillas for Palestine* (London: Portico Publications, 1976), 15.
51. AbuKhalil, *Internal Contradictions in the PFLP*, 361.
52. Khaled, *My People Shall Live*, 82.
53. Ibid., 106.
54. Rayyes and Nahas, *Guerrillas for Palestine*, 16.
55. Khaled, *My People Shall Live*, 104–6.
56. Ibid., 116.

CHAPTER 2

1. Kazziha, *Revolutionary Transformation in the Arab World*, 84.
2. Samuel M. Katz, *Israel vs Jibril: The Thirty-Year War Against a Master Terrorist* (New York: Paragon House, 1993), 24.
3. Yonah Alexander, *Palestinian Secular Terrorism* (Ardsley: Transnational Publishers, 2003), 41, 45.
4. David Macey, *Frantz Fanon: A Life* (London: Granta, 2000), 24, 295, 369; Rayyes and Nahas, *Guerrillas for Palestine*, 21.
5. Rayyes and Nahas, *Guerrillas for Palestine*, 15.
6. Khaled, *My People Shall Live*, 81.
7. MacDonald, *Shoot the Women First*, 106.
8. Khaled, *My People Shall Live*, 118.
9. MacDonald, *Shoot the Women First*, 107.
10. Khaled, *My People Shall Live*, 123.
11. Ibid., 124.
12. MacDonald, *Shoot the Women First*, 107.
13. Ibid., 109.
14. Khaled, *My People Shall Live*, 133.
15. MacDonald, *Shoot the Women First*, 110.
16. Khaled, *My People Shall Live*, 133.
17. Ibid., 135.
18. MacDonald, *Shoot the Women First*, 111.
19. Ibid., 110.
20. Khaled, *My People Shall Live*, 137.

21. MacDonald, *Shoot the Women First*, 112.
22. Khaled, *My People Shall Live*, 148.
23. Ibid., 140.
24. David Raab, *Terror in Black September: The First Eyewitness Account of the Infamous 1970 Hijackings* (New York: Palgrave Macmillan, 2007), 11.
25. Ibid., 12.
26. *Observer*, August 31, 1969.
27. MacDonald, *Shoot the Women First*, 116.
28. Khaled, *My People Shall Live*, 144.
29. *Observer*, August 31, 1969.
30. Khaled, *My People Shall Live*, 143.
31. Sayigh, *Palestinians: From Peasants to Revolutionaries*, 189.
32. *Observer*, August 31, 1969.
33. MacDonald, *Shoot the Women First*, 97, and Rosana Guber, "Um gaúcho e dezoito condores nas Ilhas Malvinas: identidade política e nação sob o autoritarismo argentino," *Mana* (Brazil), vol. 6, no. 2 (2000) (article pdf downloaded from scielo.br).
34. Khaled, *My People Shall Live*, 116.
35. Ibid., 157.
36. MacDonald, *Shoot the Women First*, 116.
37. Khaled, *My People Shall Live*, 168.
38. AbuKhalil, *Internal Contradictions in the PFLP*, 370.

CHAPTER 3

1. The idea of a Palestinian political entity had been mooted by some Palestinian and other Arab leaders since the 1950s; it was the "First Arab Summit," convened in Cairo by Nasser in 1964, which announced the founding of the PLO under the chairmanship of Ahmed Shukairy, a Palestinian diplomat who had, according to Helena Cobban, "served long years in the foreign services of Syria, Saudi Arabia and the Arab League." But riven by internal splits, criticized by a range of Palestinian groups and Arab regimes, and regarded with caution by many of the resistance organizations, the PLO remained ineffective until, heavily associated with the main Arab regimes and therefore discredited along with them by the 1967 defeat, it was effectively taken over by Fatah in 1968–69, culminating in Yasser Arafat's election as chair by the fifth Palestinian National Congress in February 1969. A unity pact signed in May 1970 by most of the resistance organizations, including the PFLP, recognized the PLO as the overarching organization of national unity for the Palestine liberation movement. Despite this, the member resistance groups continued to operate independently and at times to take decisions at odds with official PLO policy.
2. Asher Susser, *On Both Banks of the Jordan: A Political Biography of Wasfi al-Tall* (London: Frank Cass, 1994), 47–52.

3. David Pryce-Jones, *The Face of Defeat* (London: Quartet, 1974), 44.

4. Amal Kawar, *Daughters of Palestine: Leading Women of the Palestinian National Movement* (Albany: State University of New York Press, 1996), 32.

5. Pryce-Jones, *The Face of Defeat*, 45.

6. Ibid., 47.

7. Ibid., 140.

8. Khaled, *My People Shall Live*, 169.

9. Ibid., 170.

10. Kawar, *Daughters of Palestine*, 43.

11. MacDonald, *Shoot the Women First*, 100.

12. Khaled, *My People Shall Live*, 182.

13. Peter Snow and David Phillips, *Leila's Hijack War: From the Day of the Mass Hijack to the Day of Nasser's Funeral* (London: Pan Books, 1970), 79.

14. Ibid., 80.

15. Raab, *Terror in Black September*, 22.

16. Khaled, *My People Shall Live*, 187.

17. Annie Wu, "The History of Airport Security," US National Public Radio transcript, 2004, http://savvytraveler.publicradio.org/show/features/2000/20000915/security.shtml

18. Khaled, *My People Shall Live*, 185.

19. MacDonald, *Shoot the Women First*, 121.

20. Ibid.

21. Raab, *Terror in Black September*, 17.

22. Ibid., 18.

23. Ibid., 19.

24. MacDonald, *Shoot the Women First*, 122.

25. Raab, *Terror in Black September*, 19.

26. Khaled, *My People Shall Live*, 189.

27. Raab, *Terror in Black September*, 19.

28. *Guardian*, October 10, 1970.

29. Stanley Stewart, *Emergency: Crisis on the Flight Deck* (Marlborough: Airlife Publishing, 1989), 107.

30. Raab, *Terror in Black September*, 20.

31. Khaled, *My People Shall Live*, 191.

32. MacDonald, *Shoot the Women First*, 124.

33. Khaled, *My People Shall Live*, 198.

34. Stewart, *Emergency: Crisis on the Flight Deck*, 108.

35. Ibid., 109.

36. Ibid., 106.

37. Ibid., 120.

38. *Guardian*, September 13, 1970.

39. Raab, *Terror in Black September*, 29.

40. Snow and Phillips, *Leila's Hijack War*, 25.

41. Raab, *Terror in Black September*, 85.

42. Snow and Phillips, *Leila's Hijack War*, 29.
43. *Guardian*, September 10, 1970.
44. Khaled, *My People Shall Live*, 200.
45. MacDonald, *Shoot the Women First*, 129.
46. Snow and Phillips, *Leila's Hijack War*, 174.
47. MacDonald, *Shoot the Women First*, 130.
48. Snow and Phillips, *Leila's Hijack War*, 175.

CHAPTER 4

1. Rayyes and Nahas, *Guerrillas for Palestine*, 22.
2. Fisk, *Pity the Nation*, 71.
3. See, e.g., Rima Sabban in Nahid Toubia (ed.), *Women of the Arab World* (London: Zed Press, 1988), 124.
4. Markar Melkonian, *My Brother's Road: An American's Fateful Journey to Armenia* (London/New York: I. B. Tauris, 2007), 76.
5. *Guardian*, June 6, 1972.
6. AbuKhalil, *Internal Contradictions in the PFLP*, 367.
7. *Guardian*, April 3, 1978.
8. See for example Katz, *Israel vs Jibril*.
9. AbuKhalil, *Internal Contradictions in the PFLP*, 363.
10. Khaled, *My People Shall Live*, 123, 168.
11. Yukiko Miyagi, "China's Palestine Policy," unpublished CASAW workshop paper, delivered at Durham University, October 2009.
12. Bassam Abu-Sharif and Uzi Mahnaimi, *Tried by Fire: The Searing True Story of Two Men at the Heart of the Struggle Between the Arabs and the Jews* (London: Little, Brown & Co, 1995), 97.
13. *Guardian*, June 5, 1973.
14. Abu-Sharif and Mahnaimi, *Tried by Fire*, 200.
15. Julie Peteet, "Women and the Palestinian Movement: No Going Back?," in Saud Joseph and Susan Slyomovics (eds.), *Women and Power in the Middle East* (Philadelphia: University of Pennsylvania Press, 2001).

CHAPTER 5

1. Shamillah Wilson, Anasuya Sengupta and Kristy Evans, *Defending Our Dreams: Global Feminist Voices for a New Generation* (London/New York: Zed Books, 2005), 144.
2. Souad Dajani, "Between National and Social Liberation: The Palestinian Women's Movement in the Israeli Occupied West Bank and Gaza Strip," in Tamar Mayer (ed.), *Women and the Israeli Occupation: The Politics of Change* (London: Routledge, 1994), 33; and Sarah Graham-Brown,

"Women's Activism in the Middle East: A Historical Perspective," in Joseph and Slyomovics, *Women and Power in the Middle East*, 28.

3. Joseph Massad, "Conceiving the Masculine: Gender and Palestinian Nationalism," *Middle East Journal*, vol. 49, no. 3 (Summer, 1995), 467, 470–1, 474.

4. Frances Hasso, "Modernity and Gender in Arab Accounts of the 1948 and 1967 Defeats," *International Journal of Middle East Studies*, vol. 32, no. 4 (November 2000), 492.

5. Hamida Kazi, *Palestinian Women and the National Liberation Movement: A Social Perspective*, in Khamsin Collective (ed.), *Women in the Middle East* (London: Zed Books, 1987), 28.

6. Rita Giacaman and Muna Odeh, "The Palestinian Women's Movement in the Israeli-Occupied West Bank and Gaza Strip," in Toubia (ed.), *Women of the Arab World*, 58.

7. Soraya Antonius, "Fighting on Two Fronts: Conversations with Palestinian Women," *Journal of Palestine Studies*, vol. 8, no. 3 (Spring, 1979), 26–45, 36.

8. Kazi, *Palestinian Women and the National Liberation Movement*, 28.

9. Peteet in Joseph and Slyomovics (eds.), *Women and Power in the Middle East*, 136.

10. Giacaman and Odeh in Toubia (ed.), *Women of the Arab World*, 60.

11. Peteet in Joseph and Slyomovics (eds.), *Women and Power in the Middle East*, 139.

12. Peteet, "Women and the Palestinian Movement," 137.

13. Antonius, *Fighting on Two Fronts*, 28–9.

14. Abu-Sharif and Mahnaimi, *Tried by Fire*, 232–3.

15. Wenona Giles, Malathi de Alwis, Edith Klein and Neluka Silva (eds.), *Feminists Under Fire: Exchanges Across War Zones* (Toronto: Between the Lines, 2003), 1.

16. Ibid., 11.

17. See, e.g., Morgan, *The Demon Lover*.

18. See, e.g., Dajani, "Between National and Social Liberation," 33–61; also Rita Giacaman, Islah Jad, and Penny Johnson, "For the Common Good? Gender and Social Citizenship in Palestine," and Rita Giacaman and Penny Johnson, "Searching for Strategies: The Palestinian Women's Movement in the New Era," both in Joseph and Slyomovics, *Women and Power in the Middle East*, 126–34 and 150–8.

19. Kawar, *Daughters of Palestine*, 58–9.

20. Miyagi, "China's Palestine Policy."

21. This incident is—minus the nudity—very similar to a scene in the 2008 German film *The Baader-Meinhof Complex*, where a group of Red Army Faction activists visit the training camp of an unnamed Palestinian revolutionary group and are expelled for public nudity and sexual activity. The tension between Palestinian sexual conservatism and the supposedly emancipated sexuality of the 1970s European and American left is a

recurrent theme in Western and Israeli writings on the 1970s Palestinian left and in related fiction, such as John Le Carre's *Little Drummer Girl*.

22. *Guardian*, July 18, 1980.
23. Morgan, *The Demon Lover*, 209–10.
24. Kawar, *Daughters of Palestine*, 62.
25. *Guardian*, July 18, 1980.
26. Aitemad Muhanna, "The Leftist and Islamic Movements in Gaza: Conflating Ideology and Practice?," unpublished conference paper delivered at the School of Oriental and African Studies, February 27–28, 2010; see also page 126 of this volume.
27. Antonius, *Fighting on Two Fronts*, 30.
28. Ibid., 33.
29. Alexander, *Palestinian Secular Terrorism*, 33.
30. Kazziha, *Revolutionary Transformation in the Arab World*, 23.
31. Alexander, *Palestinian Secular Terrorism*, 38.
32. Sayigh, *Palestinians: From Peasants to Revolutionaries*, 165.
33. Ibid., 180.
34. Kawar, *Daughters of Palestine*, 85–6.
35. Amal Kawar, "Palestinian Women's Activism after Oslo," in Suha Sabbagh (ed.), *Palestinian Women of Gaza and the West Bank* (Indianapolis: Indiana University Press, 1998), 239.
36. Said K. Aburish, *Arafat: From Defender to Dictator* (London: Bloomsbury, 1998).
37. Joost Hiltermann, "The Women's Movement During the Uprising," in Sabbagh (ed.), *Palestinian Women of Gaza and the West Bank*, 41, 41–52, 42–3.
38. www.upwc.org.ps, August 1, 2011.
39. "Union of Palestinian Women's Committees: Farewell to Comrade Leader Maha Nassar," www.pflp.ps, October 14, 2008.
40. Kawar, *Daughters of Palestine*, 103.
41. Ibid., 102.
42. Giacaman and Johnson, "Searching for Strategies," 156.

CHAPTER 6

1. "'This Calm Will Not Last': Jon Elmer Interviews Palestinian Icon Leila Khaled," IPS News Service, November 4, 2009.
2. See, for instance, "Jailed PFLP leader: Only a One-State Solution is Possible," *Ha'aretz*, May 5 2010, http://www.haaretz.com/news/diplomacy-defense/jailed-pflp-leader-only-a-one-state-solution-is-possible-1.288412
3. "A Just Solution is the Way Out of Conflict," *An Phoblacht*, August 11, 2005.
4. *New York Times*, February 20, 1996.
5. *Guardian*, April 22, 1987.

6. "'This Calm Will Not Last'," IPS News Service, November 4, 2009.
7. Joel Beinin, "The Israeli-Palestinian Conflict and the Arab Awakening," *Middle East Report Online*, August 1, 2011.
8. "An Interview with Khalida Jarrar of the Popular Front for the Liberation of Palestine (PFLP)," Alternative Information Centre, May 12, 2009.
9. Joe Stork, *Erased in a Moment: Suicide Bombing Attacks Against Israeli civilians* (New York: Human Rights Watch, 2002), 89.
10. Taped interview by Mike Walker, April 6, 2010, transcript and YouTube video link via http://wpnz-pflp-solidarity.blogspot.com
11. Greg Philo and Mike Berry, *Bad News From Israel* (London: Pluto Press, 2004).
12. http://www.btselem.org/English/Statistics/Casualties.asp
13. Barbara Victor, *Army of Roses: Inside the World of Palestinian Women Suicide Bombers* (London: Constable and Robinson, 2004), 142.
14. Ibid., 63.
15. Giacaman, Jad and Johnson, "For the Common Good? Gender and Social Citizenship in Palestine," 146.
16. Kawar, *Daughters of Palestine*, 115–17.
17. Muhanna, "The Leftist and Islamic Movements in Gaza."
18. "What Makes a Woman go to War?," www.rt.com, May 20, 2011.
19. Kawar, *Daughters of Palestine*, 117.
20. Khaled Hroub, *Hamas: A Beginner's Guide* (London/Ann Arbor: Pluto Press, 2006), 76–7.

CHAPTER 7

1. "Palestine on the Table at World Social Forum in Kenya," Palestine News Network, January 24, 2007.
2. "A Just Solution is the Way Out of Conflict," *An Phoblacht*, August 11, 2005.
3. "Comrade Leila Khaled Meets with Nicaraguan President Ortega," www.pflp.ps, November 2010.
4. "Former Palestinian Guerrilla Commander Khaled in Mersin," Firat News Agency, June 4, 2011.
5. "Something Rotten in Sweden," www.ynetnews.com, May 6, 2011.
6. "Messaggi di solidarietà alla FIOM da organismi internazionali," www.carc.it, October 15, 2010.
7. Beinin, "The Israeli-Palestinian Conflict and the Arab Awakening."
8. Jesse Rosenfeld and Joseph Dana, "A Palestinian Revolt in the Making?," *The Nation*, May 26, 2011.
9. Beinin, "The Israeli-Palestinian Conflict and the Arab Awakening."
10. Ahmed Moor, "Learning From Leila," *This Week in Palestine*, April 2011.
11. "BDS Breaking New Barriers," *Al-Ahram Weekly*, May 4, 2011.
12. Morgan, *The Demon Lover*, 209.
13. US Palestinian Community Network, http://whenireturn.uspcn.org

Bibliography and Sources

A large proportion of the information about Leila Khaled's life laid out in this book is drawn from a week of interviews I conducted with her in her Home in Amman, Jordan, in September 2008 and by email and Skype between then and November 2011. Where information and quotations from Khaled are not otherwise referenced, this is the source. Undated references from Khalil Meqdisi of the PFLP's English Language Unit are drawn from a telephone interview with him conducted in September 2009, and comments and information from Linda Clair are from an interview in July 2008. A number of comments and items of information are also included from Palestinian men and women who preferred to remain anonymous: the bulk of these are drawn from conversations and interviews conducted in the West Bank and Israel in January 2008 and March–April 2009 or in Manchester in 2009.

PUBLISHED SOURCES

AbuKhalil, As'ad, "Internal Contradictions in the PFLP: Decision Making and Policy Determination," *Middle East Journal*, vol. 41, no. 3 (Summer 1987).

Aburish, Said K., *Arafat: From Defender to Dictator* (London: Bloomsbury, 1998).

Abu-Sharif, Bassam and Uzi Mahnaimi, *Tried by Fire: The Searing True Story of Two Men at the Heart of the Struggle Between the Arabs and the Jews* (London: Little, Brown & Co., 1995).

Afzal-Khan, Fawzia, "Bridging the Gap Between So-Called Postcolonial and Minority Women of Color: A Comparative Methodology for Third World Feminist Literary Criticism," *Womanist Theory and Research*, vol. 2.1– 2.2 (1996–97).

Ahmad, Eqbal and David Barsamian, *Terrorism: Theirs and Ours* (New York: Seven Stories Press, 2001).

Alexander, Yonah, *Palestinian Secular Terrorism* (Ardsley: Transnational Publishers, 2003).

Antonius, Soraya, "Fighting on Two Fronts: Conversations with Palestinian Women," *Journal of Palestine Studies*, vol. 8, no. 3 (Spring 1979), 26–45.

Ashrawi, Hanan, *This Side of Peace: A Personal Account* (London: Simon & Schuster, 1995).

Bechara, Soha, *Resistance: My Life for Lebanon* (New York: Soft Skull Press, 2003).

Buck-Morss, Susan, *Thinking Past Terror: Islamism and Critical Theory on the Left* (London/New York: Verso, 2003).

Cobban, Helena, *The Palestinian Liberation Organisation: People, Power and Politics* (Cambridge: Cambridge University Press, 1984).

Cooley, John K., *Green March, Black September: The Story of the Palestinian Arabs* (London: Frank Cass, 1973).

Dawisha, Adeed, *Arab Nationalism in the Twentieth Century: From Triumph to Despair* (Princeton: Princeton University Press, 2003).

Emerson, Steven and Brian Duffy, *The Fall of Pan Am 103* (London: Futura, 1990).

Fisk, Robert, *Pity the Nation: Lebanon at War* (Oxford: Oxford University Press, 1990/2001).

Gilbert, Martin, *Israel: A History* (London: Doubleday, 1998).

Giles, Wenona, Malathi de Alwis, Edith Klein, and Neluka Silva (eds.), *Feminists Under Fire: Exchanges Across War Zones* (Toronto: Between the Lines, 2003).

Grace, Daphne, *The Woman in the Muslin Mask: Veiling and Identity in Postcolonial Literature* (London/Sterling: Pluto Press, 2004).

Gresh, Alain, *The PLO: The Struggle Within* (London: Zed Books, 1983).

Habache, Georges and Georges Malbrunot, *Les revolutionnaires ne meurent jamais: conversations avec Georges Malbrunot* (Paris: Editions Fayard, 2008).

Hasso, Frances, "Modernity and Gender in Arab Accounts of the 1948 and 1967 Defeats," *International Journal of Middle East Studies*, vol. 32, no. 4 (Nov 2000), 491–510.

Holt, Maria, *Women in Contemporary Palestine* (Jerusalem: PASSIA, 1996).

Hourani, Albert, *A History of the Arab Peoples* (London: Faber & Faber, 1991).

Hroub, Khaled, *Hamas: A Beginner's Guide* (London/Ann Arbor: Pluto Press, 2006).

Joseph, Suad and Susan Slyomovics (eds.), *Women and Power in the Middle East* (Philadelphia: University of Pennsylvania Press, 2001).

Kadi, Leila S. (ed./trans.), *Basic Political Documents of the Armed Palestinian Resistance Movement* (Beirut: PLO Research Center [Palestine Books No. 27], 1969).

Karanjia, R. K., *Arab Dawn* (London: Lawrence & Wishart, 1959).

Katz, Samuel M. *Israel vs Jibril: The Thirty-Year War Against a Master Terrorist* (New York: Paragon House, 1993).

Kawar, Amal, *Daughters of Palestine: Leading Women of the Palestinian National Movement* (Albany: State University of New York Press, 1996).

Kazziha, Walid, *Revolutionary Transformation in the Arab World: Habash and his Comrades From Nationalism to Marxism* (London/Tonbridge: Charles Knight & Co., 1975).

Khaled, Leila and George Hajjar, *My People Shall Live: The Autobiography of a Revolutionary* (London: Hodder & Stoughton, 1973).

Khamsin Collective (ed.), *Women in the Middle East* (London: Zed Books, 1987).

Kharmi, Ghada, *In Search of Fatima: A Palestinian Story* (London/New York: Verso, 2002).

Khoury, Rana, *Palestinian Women and the Intifada* (Bethlehem: International Center of Bethlehem Department of Women's Studies, 1995).

Lewis, Reina, *Gendering Orientalism: Race, Femininity and Representation* (London/New York: Routledge, 1986).

McCullin, Don, *Unreasonable Behaviour: An Autobiography* (London: Vintage, 1990).

MacDonald, Eileen, *Shoot the Women First* (London: Arrow Books, 1991).

Macey, David, *Frantz Fanon: A Life* (London: Granta, 2000).

McGowan, Daniel and Marc H. Ellis, *Remembering Deir Yassin: The Future of Israel and Palestine* (New York: Olive Branch Press, 1998).

Massad, Joseph, "Conceiving the Masculine: Gender and Palestinian Nationalism," *Middle East Journal*, vol. 49, no. 3 (Summer 1995), 467.

Mayer, Tamar (ed.), *Women and the Israeli Occupation: The Politics of Change* (London/New York: Routledge, 1994).

Melkonian, Markar, *My Brother's Road: An American's Fateful Journey to Armenia* (London/New York: I. B. Tauris, 2007).

Morgan, Robin, *The Demon Lover: On the Sexuality of Terrorism* (London: Mandarin, 1989).

Morris, Benny (ed.), *Making Israel* (Ann Arbor: University of Michigan Press, 2007).

Najjar, Alexandre, *The School of War* (London: Telegram, 1999/2006).

Owen, Roger, *State, Power and Politics in the Making of the Modern Middle East* (London/New York: Routledge, 1992).

Pappe, Ilan, *The Ethnic Cleansing of Palestine* (Oxford: Oneworld Publications, 2006).

Philo, Greg and Mike Berry, *Bad News from Israel* (London: Pluto Press, 2004).

Pryce-Jones, David, *The Face of Defeat* (London: Quartet, 1974).

Raab, David, *Terror in Black September: The First Eyewitness Account of the Infamous 1970 Hijackings* (New York: Palgrave Macmillan, 2007).

El-Rayyes, Riad and Dunia Nahas, *Guerrillas for Palestine* (London: Portico Publications, 1976).

Rogers, Mary Eliza, *Domestic Life in Palestine* (London: Kegan Paul, 1862/1989).

Rothschild, John (ed.), *Forbidden Agendas: Intolerance and Defiance in the Middle East: Writings From the Journal Khamsin* (London: Al Saqi Books, 1984).

El Saadawi, Nawal, *A Daughter of Isis: The Autobiography of Nawal El Saadawi* (London/New York: Zed Books, 1999).

Sabbagh, Suha, *Palestinian Women of Gaza and the West Bank* (Bloomington and Indianapolis: Indiana University Press, 1998).

Said, Edward, *Peace and its Discontents: Gaza-Jericho 1993–1995* (London: Vintage, 1995).

Said, Edward, *Out of Place: A Memoir* (London: Granta, 1999).

Sayigh, Rosemary, *Palestinians: From Peasants to Revolutionaries* (London: Zed Books, 1979).

Segev, Tom, *One Palestine, Complete: Jews and Arabs Under the British Mandate* (New York: Henry Holt & Co., 1999).

Snow, Peter and David Phillips, *Leila's Hijack War: From the Day of the Mass Hijack to the Day of Nasser's Funeral* (London: Pan Books, 1970).

Stewart, Stanley, *Emergency: Crisis on the Flight Deck* (Marlborough: Airlife Publishing, 1989).

Stork, Joe, *Erased in a Moment: Suicide Bombing Attacks Against Israeli Civilians* (New York: Human Rights Watch, 2002).

Susser, Asher, *On Both Banks of the Jordan: A Political Biography of Wasfi al-Tall* (London: Frank Cass, 1994).

Toubia, Nahid (ed.), *Women of the Arab World: The Coming Challenge* (London: Zed Books, 1988).

Victor, Barbara, *Army of Roses: Inside the World of Palestinian Women Suicide Bombers* (London: Constable & Robinson, 2004).

Wilson, Shamillah, Anasuya Sengupta, and Kristy Evans, *Defending Our Dreams: Global Feminist Voices for a New Generation* (London/New York: Zed Books, 2005).

Wu, Annie, "The History of Airport Security," US National Public Radio transcript, 2004; http://savvytraveler.publicradio.org/show/features/2000/20000915/security.shtml

OTHER SOURCES

B'Tselem (Israeli human rights organization); http://www.btselem.org/English

Guardian/Observer newspaper digital archive 1791–2000; http://archive.guardian.co.uk

Makboul, Lina (director), *Leila Khaled: Hijacker* (documentary), Swedish Television, Nederland NPS; www.leilakhaled.com

Miyagi, Yukiko, "China's Palestine Policy," unpublished CASAW workshop paper, delivered at Durham University, October 2009.

Muhanna, Aitemad, "The Leftist and Islamic Movements in Gaza: Conflating Ideology and Practice?," unpublished conference paper delivered at the School of Oriental and African Studies, February 27–8, 2010.

Index